Praise for *Carry a Paintbrush*

"Once you begin *Carry A Paintbrush* you won't want to put it, or your Paintbrush down. Both open possibilities to the life you may have always imagined for yourself, but may not have known how to achieve. Susanne Goldstein can teach it because she has lived it. At a time when the future and how we fit in it seems more confusing than ever, along comes this very practical volume that combines personal wisdom and professional experience to paint an irresistibly inviting portrait of the career success that awaits you."

-Billy Shore, Author and Founder &
Executive Director, Share Our Strength

Susanne Goldstein's brilliant manifesto is a MUST READ for anyone who has either painted their career into a corner, or is just starting out. In this book are all the tools you'll need to get unstuck and create a career of your own design.

-Stephen M. Shapiro, Author, *Goal-Free Living* and
Personality Poker

"Colleges prepare students for everything academic and very little that is practical. Students graduate having very little idea about what they want to do in life and even less of an idea about how to go about getting what they want. Where do they turn for practical wisdom on what to do next and how to do it? Susanne Goldstein's book is meant to help these lost souls. She has prepared a set of well written pieces of advice about how to find out who you are and what you want and how to go about getting it. This book should be part of every new college graduate's library."

-Roger Schank, John Evans Professor Emeritus in computer science, education and psychology at Northwestern University

"Forget career development – how about career inspiration? If you are going to buy only one book on how to get the most out of your work life, this is the one you want to get and actually read."

-David L. Norris, CEO, BlueCava and expert on
entrepreneurship

Carry a Paintbrush

Carry a Paintbrush

How to Be the Artistic Director of Your Own Career

Susanne Goldstein

Carry A Paintbrush
How to Be the Artistic Director of Your Own Career

ISBN 978-0-615-44926-5

10 9 8 7 6 5 4 3 2

For more information:

info@carryapaintbrush.com
www.carryapaintbrush.com

Life is like a game of cards. The hand that is dealt you represents determinism; the way you play it is free will.

- Jawaharlal Nehru

To my parents Art & Vida Goldstein

and to my mentor David Squire

CONTENTS

Part 4

Paint Yourself into the Picture:
Be Prepared When Luck Strikes

Part 5

Nurture Your Inner Career Artist:
Let Yourself Evolve

Acknowledgments

One of the lessons you'll learn in this book is that creating the career you've always wanted is a *team sport*. So, I have learned, is writing a book.

These people are my team, and I'd like to acknowledge and thank them for their support, enthusiasm and hard work.

The Parents: Even down to the final proofread, my parents Art and Vida Goldstein have given me the gift of their love and support.

The Mentor: You wouldn't be reading this book if David Squire hasn't insisted (in the most loving way, of course) that I write it.

The Best Friend/Book Guru: I couldn't imagine going through this process without the love, support and brilliant counsel of Stephen Shapiro.

The Other First Time Author: I sat in silence for hours and hours writing next to the incomparable Verna Myers. We did it!

The Editors: A huge shout out to the ladies at WordsRU.com. Candace, I know how far above and beyond you went for me, and your fingerprints can be seen all over this book. I wish I could thank you properly. Jeanmarie, thanks for all of your support.

The Designer: After fifteen years of working together, true friend and genius cover and website designer, Steve de Brun still blows me away with his talent.

The Members of Team Paintbrush: Erik Gregory, Sebastian Moscardi, Ligia Buzan, Elizabeth Carr, Kristin Canders, Gustavo Lanzas, David Norris, and Alex Kjerulf have all worked behind the scenes to make the book, the website, the workshops and webinars possible. They've also kept me sane. Thanks to all of you for believing. I hope we all get to work together for a long, long time.

The Social Network: To my Facebook friends and fans – your daily encouragement continues to be priceless.

Prologue

Why Now? Why This Book?

On a bright day in March, I had a chat with an author friend. He was helping me prepare for my first big interview about this book, and we were doing a mock interview session, he being the interviewer, and me being, well, me.

"I really, really don't want to blow this. Please tell me how not to really, really blow this!"

So he did.

"There are two things you need to know about talking about your book," he said.

"First, you need to know how to answer the question "why now?" Why is right now the right time for this book?

And second, you need to know the answer to the question "why this book?" What makes this book required reading for every job searcher out there?"

Why now?

The "why now?" question was easy. Never before in my life have I seen so many people despondent over their career prospects. Years of high unemployment and low economic confidence were making even the most positive Pollyanna into a naysayer.

Yet, I knew there were still great jobs out there to be had. It was just a question of finding out how to gain *access* to them. And here's the answer to "why now?"

In the twenty-first century, "access" to *access* has completely changed.

In the *old world*, access was limited to the privileged few who had money or the family connections to open doors and obtain it. When the economy was chugging along and jobs were plentiful, access itself wasn't very important. But when times were rough, and jobs were scarce, access mattered an awful lot.

In the *new world*, the world of uber connectivity, online social networks and offline Meetups, access is much more available and attainable. Technology has enabled us to be more connected than ever. And with that connectedness, our mindset about meeting and helping new people (both off- and online) has completely changed.

No longer is your circle of contacts limited to *who you know;* it's now expanded to *who you know **knows**,* and *who those people know* as well. This network of connections provides an opportunity for those without prior access to have it.

There's nowhere more appropriate to apply this new connectedness than in the world of job hunting and career development.

This book is full of techniques, stories and teachings that demonstrate how to engage these off- and online networks to your best advantage. It couldn't have been written until these channels of connectivity had been opened. And that answers the "why now?"

Why This Book?

For more than two decades, I have been inventing and reinventing myself, designing and bringing a wide variety of products to market. From theatrical plays and Hollywood movies, to course curricula, software applications and websites, I've become expert in helping people and teams *define, design, develop and market great products.*

This book will teach you that your career is an extremely important product that you need to *define, develop, and market.*

Okay, that may sound a little harsh. But the truth is that career development is a deeply personal and often painful process. I believe that the best way to take the charge off of the emotions surrounding career development is to *apply structured thinking.* That's what this book does.

If you are feeling stuck, or lost, or out of control in your career, this book will get you back on track.

By focusing on the process of career development, you will understand who you are, where you want to go and how to get there.

The techniques in this book aren't built on theory.

They are the practical methods I have been using throughout my career to create my own dynamic working life. I've met, networked with, and befriended hundreds of people. I've envisioned what I wanted to do, and found creative, unexpected ways of getting there. I've worked hard, and was lucky. And I kept landing job after cool job.

As I did this, friends and colleagues started taking note. They started asking me for advice on how they could do the same for themselves.

Pulling from my own stories and my varied product development experiences, I started coaching people on how they could use creative thinking and networking to take control of their working lives.

I observed that the more my coaching clients committed to these methods, the more successful they became. It seemed that I was on to something. So I created a set of career development tools that, just like those used in traditional product development, helped my clients define, design and bring *themselves* to market.

This book represents fifteen years of real-life stories and proven practices that have allowed enabled my clients to succeed in creating the careers they've always wanted.

I call this process *Carry a Paintbrush,* and if you grab your own paintbrush and commit to the techniques in this book, I promise you'll never look at your working life the same way again. I hope you enjoy the journey.

Susanne Goldstein
Boston, Massachusetts
Spring, 2011

Introduction

Confessions of a Career Artist

My name is Susanne Goldstein, and I am a Career Artist. My tools are an imaginary bucket of Paint and a Paintbrush. For twenty-five years I've been designing my own future, creating opportunities for luck to happen, and inventing jobs where none had previously existed.

I found my Paintbrush for the first time during the summer between my two senior years in college. During the junior year of my mechanical engineering program at Cornell University, I realized that I was only three credits away from an additional degree in theater and film studies. Knowing no better, and having been born with a fair amount of *chutzpah*, I approached the head of the liberal arts department with a proposal for creating an independent major that would get me a bachelor of arts degree in conjunction with my bachelor of science degree.

The deal I struck with the head of the liberal arts college was as follows:

1) I would fulfill a language requirement

2) I would take an advanced filmmaking class

3) I would spend a semester abroad to get experience working in the theater.

So upon completion of the first of my two senior years, bags packed, and a six-month student visa in hand, I headed to London. Next on the agenda was to find a theater job that would fulfill my "experience" requirement with the folks back in Ithaca.

I had never thought much about the expression, "necessity is the mother of all invention." Fresh out of college, bright-eyed and bushy-tailed, I had no idea how to find a job, get a job, or keep a job. And I needed one. Unfortunately, they don't teach you these kinds of things in thermodynamics class nor in "Lessons from the Greek Tragedies." But, knowing I needed to get it done, I set out to find some "experience."

For those of you who don't know, London is truly the hub of theater activity in the world. Between the West End's (think Broadway) enormous playhouses to the Fringe's (think off- and off-off Broadway) multitude of large and small stages, London is full of theaters. But, determined youngster that I was, I decided that the only place I was willing to get my "experience" in London was at the world famous National Theatre of Great Britain.[1]

The best thing about being young and foolish is that you are, by definition, young and foolish. Unencumbered by etiquette, appropriateness or rules, an ambitious youthful Fool is hard to stop. I was such a Fool.

Determined to work at "The National," and knowing the name of one person who worked there (before the Internet, this wasn't as easy as you might think), I set out to get a job. What job, you ask? I had no idea. There was no job. There was no job listing. To the more informed and less delusional, this really must have seemed insane. But I was bound and

---

[1] Since my time at The National, it has been granted a royal charter and is now known as the Royal National Theatre of Great Britain.

determined to work there and for me, there was no other option.

So I did what I could to prepare for a job I knew nothing about, working for a person I didn't know. I tucked into my book bag a paper I had written on class struggles in Arthur Miller plays and some blueprints for a house I designed as a project for a solar engineering class. I brought a list of theater courses I had taken, plays I had been involved with, and a résumé of my completely unrelated prior summer work experience. And then I hit the road. Well, the lobby actually.

It wasn't until years later that I named the phenomenon in my life that I call the Paintbrush. Maybe the Paintbrush was born from being immersed in the creative environment of the theater department or the inventive, problem-solving atmosphere of the engineering school. Whatever the case, at that moment, when I walked into the lobby of The National Theatre of Great Britain, the Paintbrush was born.

So what happened exactly? One cheery morning, happy and smiling and oh-so-American, I waltzed into the National's backstage lobby and presented myself to the woman behind the reception desk.

"Hello," I said. "My name is Susanne Goldstein. I'm an American student taking a semester abroad, and I'm interested in getting a job here at The National."

Now honestly, I'm not sure this woman had ever seen anyone quite like me. Blonde and brazen, yet polite and well-spoken, I fear she just didn't know what to make of me.

"I'm terribly sorry," she said in her lovely English lilt, "but do you have an appointment?"

"No, I don't," I replied. "But I do know the name Kevin Cahill, or perhaps you can me tell whom I might speak to about a job? Do you think you might be able to help me?"

"We're very busy here," she replied, "and I would have to look into that for you. But I'm occupied at the moment. You wouldn't mind coming back later, would you?"

"If it's okay with you," I said, "I'll wait."

And so I did. Every day for almost two weeks I would show up at the lobby and wait for the receptionists to help me find someone to talk to. When things were slow, I would chat with them, asking questions about the NT, collecting brochures and reading cast and crew bios from the playbills. Sometimes I would bring them tea. I was patient. And kind. And not in the way. And persistent.

I think it was on the eighth day of waiting that the miracle happened. Kevin Cahill and Jason Barnes agreed to speak with me. It turned out that Jason needed to hire an assistant production manager for one of the NT's three stages—someone who was knowledgeable in theater, skilled in mechanical drafting, and who was a hard worker. That was me! And the next day, I got the job.

What I realized I had done at that moment was "Paint a Door." Painting Doors, then opening and walking through them has been the basis for how I have built my career, and one of the many practical techniques that you will learn in this book.

Metaphorically speaking, I like to think that I always carry with me a Bucket of Paint and a Paintbrush. When I see something interesting that I want to learn about, experience, or engage with, I take out my Paintbrush, Paint a Door, open it, and walk through.

Think of Painting Doors as Creating Opportunities for Luck to Happen. This book is about how you can understand your own wants and desires in life and translate those into doors that you can paint and then open.

Door opening is a scary proposition for many people. My hope in writing this book is to share with you some stories and tools that will help you identify opportunities, paint doors and create for yourself the type of career you've always dreamed of having.

Part 1

Create Your Own Career:
Claim Your Career as Your Own

Man does not simply exist, but always decides what his existence will be, what he will become in the next moment.

- Viktor Frankl

Chapter 1

You Too Can Be a Career Artist

Okay, I have another confession to make. When I started out on the journey that would become my career, I had absolutely no idea what I was doing. Really. But somehow, I've been able to figure it out and do some pretty cool things.

I'm very aware that some of the stories and techniques in this book might push you out of your comfort zone.

Much of what you are going to read is going to ask you to rethink the way you are in the world. So I'm going to ask you to have a little faith. The techniques in this book work, and if you can suspend your discomfort for about 200 pages, I can pretty much guarantee that you will never look at your career and your work the same way again.

So let's get started.

When I try to explain to people what I do for a living, I am, quite honestly, often stumped. The wanderings of my career have taken me from professional theater to film producing and writing, to technical writing, and to interactive TV design. At the beginning of the Dotcom era, I found myself in Silicon Valley designing user interfaces for this new thing called the World Wide Web, despite the fact that I had no idea what I was doing. From there I have grown my "business" to include product development, product marketing, user experience design, project management, online and direct marketing, executive coaching, small business advising, and career counseling. Trust me, there is no easy way to put all of that on a business card.

To an outsider, the mish-mash of my career might not make any sense. But it makes all of the sense in the world to me. My career has followed the organic evolution of who I am as a person, and what I've wanted to do for a living.

I suppose I am sort of like a frog, and I've spent my career jumping from lily pad to lily pad, learning, creating, and experiencing along the way.

So how did I do this? And more importantly, how can you do this? As I said earlier, in the beginning, I had no idea what I was doing. What I did have, was an idea of what I wanted, and a willingness to try a million ways to get there.

The problem was that I didn't learn these things in college. I had to figure it out for myself.

Lucky for me, I was born with a fair share of industriousness, persistence, and creativity. Lucky for you, even if you were born without some of these traits, even if you have no idea where to start, I've figured it out for you.

The frameworks and techniques in this book will help you learn how to be the Artistic Director of Your Own Career. Whether you are a Career Starter, a Career Transitioner or a Solo-Practitioner, this book will provide you with the tools to get you there.

Here are the five basic techniques:

1. Claim Your Career as Your Own

Careers don't just happen. They are made. And it will take work on your part to create one that fulfills you, keeps you fed and warm, and allows you to grow as an individual. Until you are ready to take charge of, and *own* your career, you won't have one. You'll just have a job. In this book, you will learn how to Claim Your Career as Your Own, and then craft it into the life path that you've always wanted.

2. Know Who and What You Want to Be

A friend suggested that a great way to live life is to "set a direction and then meander with purpose." Before you step onto the path that will be your career life, you need to know *who you are* and *what you want to be*. Through example stories and exercises, you'll learn how to develop your work personality, or Personal Career Brand. With this essential tool, you can start painting and opening doors into your future.

3. Create Opportunities for Luck to Happen

Luck doesn't just happen. In his 2003 book, The Luck Factor, Richard Wiseman writes, "Luck is not a magical ability or a gift from the gods." He argues that only 10 percent of luck is truly random. The remaining 90 percent is "actually defined by the way you think."

If you ask most successful people, be they musicians, politicians, doctors, entrepreneurs, or entertainers, they will usually say that they have just been incredibly lucky. But the secret that most people don't know is that their luck didn't come out of nowhere.

True luck comes from the hard work or what I call Creating Opportunities for Luck to Happen. The entrepreneur whose company had an incredibly successful IPO (initial public offering) didn't just get lucky and build a company that people wanted a piece of. She worked long hours, built the right team, created a smart, differentiated product that people wanted, and grew to it profitability, all before the public had any interest in owning a piece of the pie.

Gordon Sumner, popularly known as the musician Sting, worked as a ditch digger, an English teacher, and a tax officer to make a living while writing and recording demos, playing in small venues, and networking like crazy. He was almost thirty years old before his hard work paid off and his band, The Police, "made it."

Creating Opportunities for Luck to Happen takes hard work, boldness, and perseverance. This book will show you how to meet the people and create the situations that will forever change your career

4. Be Prepared When Luck Strikes

How many times have you, or someone else you've known, gone into a job interview and *not* landed the job? Considering the number of applicants per job, and the scarcity of jobs, I'm pretty sure if it hasn't happened to you, it has happened to someone you know.

So who's the one who got "lucky" and landed the gig? Honestly, the chosen one wasn't lucky at all. He was *prepared*, amiable, inquisitive, *prepared*, enthusiastic, ready with ideas, *prepared*, engaging, a great person, and, oh, did I mention *prepared*?

The fact of the matter is that in general, people *buy* people. By being appropriately prepared, you more likely to make a "personal connection" with the people you are meeting, networking, or interviewing with. These personal connections make all the difference in the world. I'm going to show you how easy it is to get people to invest in *your* future and become your advocate—in both business and life.

5. Let Your Career Evolve

Human beings are not static. We are constantly evolving our interests, expanding our horizons, and taking on new challenges. Or at least that's what we're built to do. With enormous processing power up in that noggin of yours, it would be a terrible waste if you ended up doing the same thing, every day for the rest of your life.

The problem is that most of us are terrified of change. Especially as it pertains to work. Society has indoctrinated us into believing that having a secure job is the most important thing in the world. But a secure job today isn't what it once was, and as the nature of work continues to change, we must change, too.

Change can mean anything from a shift within an organization, to a change to another company, or to a change to a completely different line of work. Together, we'll investigate how and when changing is the right thing for you to do.

So let's get started. I encourage you to grab your Bucket of Paint and your Paintbrush and join me in creating the career you've always wanted.

Chapter 2

Claim Your Career as Your Own

Okay, so where to start? This is going to sound all self-help-y, but the first step in developing your inner Career Artist, is to believe. Believe that you are the owner of your career, and that you have the ability and power to make choices and decisions that will allow you to be most happy and successful. By making this claim, by owning this belief, you can stop being a victim of the job market, stop paying attention to family pressures, and begin figuring out who *you* want to be in the world. The first step requires that you have to have some belief that this system *will* work for you.

This is no easy task. So many of us have been programmed to do a certain thing, think a certain way, and follow a certain career path.

It's no surprise that entertainers have children who are entertainers, doctors beget doctors, jewelers raise the next generation of jewelers, and so on. Kids grow up around their parents and their work. What they are exposed to, what they learn about, is what they see their parents doing.

My brothers and I used to sometimes go to the office with my dad when he had to work on Saturdays, and it's no surprise that we have all grown into business people. Business, problem solving, and entrepreneurialism is what we were exposed to, and an orientation that carried over into the way my mom and dad raised us.

During family dinners, my parents would lead us in a game of "finger on the button," a quiz game where they would make up questions for us to answer. Though the topics varied—math, science, history—there was always an orientation of competition and getting ahead.

Not exactly the typical dinner table talk, I know. But the main point is that, as a result of this kind of exposure to these *business-type* principles, my folks expected us to become business people.

You can imagine their surprise when I wanted to go into the arts. Art was no way to make a living. And it certainly wasn't business.

But early on, I had discovered the types of thinking, creativity, and experiences that made *me* feel the most alive. I decided to Claim My Career as My Own and resist doing what I was supposed to do.

It was a risk. I understood that. But owning your own career doesn't necessarily mean you're going down the easiest path possible. It means that you intend to create the most satisfying path possible.

So here's what I'd like you to do.

In a moment, I want you to put down this book, look up at the sky, ceiling, out a window, or in a mirror, and say out loud, "I Claim My Career as My Own." Yeah, I know, it's totally hokey, but think of it as a symbolic act that will help you kick-start this journey.

Better yet, go to my website www.carryapaintbrush.com and make the Claim right from the homepage. There you'll find a *pledge form* where you can substantiate your Claim.

Okay, I'll wait. Put down the book. I'll be right here waiting when you come back.

Chapter 3

Creating a Career in an Unpredictable Job Market

I want to start this chapter off by thanking my parents. Thanks Mom and Dad! In the mid-80s, I was graduating with degrees in mechanical engineering *and* in theater and film studies. It was a gorgeous spring Sunday, and I was having "that" conversation with my folks again. Here's what Dad had to say:

"Susanne, there are recruiters from some of the best companies in the world coming to campus. You're a female engineer and that makes you a very desirable as a candidate. There aren't a lot of female engineers. You should go and meet with them."

"Dad, I don't want to work as an engineer. I want to work in the arts."

For my dad, hearing this must have been like eating bad seafood. He was the CEO of an international company. By the time he retired, he had been with that company for forty-three years. His perspective, to say the least, was pretty different from mine.

"Susanne, you can always do the arts on the side as a hobby," Mom said. "You should interview. If you get a job, you'll have security, a regular paycheck, and a way up the ladder."

YUCK! I couldn't imagine any scenario worse than what my mom had just described. The idea of working for one company for the rest of my life literally sucked the oxygen out of my lungs. This was the sixth or seventh time we had had this conversation, and it always ended the same way.

"I can't do it. I just can't."

"Well," my dad said, *"are you really prepared to look for a job for the rest of your life?* Because that's what it will be like for you, working in the arts."

My parents were right. I have been looking for a job every day of my life because that is the career path I have chosen. And I do it with fun, determination, and gusto.

What's more interesting though, is the fact that twenty-something years later, *most of us are now looking for jobs on a regular basis.*

The character of work has changed in the years that I've been building a career. More and more people are searching to achieve a particular balance between money and meaning in their work-life.

In his book entitled, *The Future of Work*, MIT Professor of Management, Thomas Malone, writes that the state of work, very much like the state of government, has undergone radical transformation, and is still in the process of changing. Just like the democratic revolutions of the 18th century, the major changes are occurring as a result of people recognizing what kind of freedoms they really want or should have at work.

At the heart of these changes are people just like you and me. Many of us are no longer satisfied with being the "company man." Instead, we want to carve a career path that allows us to grow, live a balanced life, and stay inspired. In other words, we're getting pickier about what we want to do for a living.

Want to Learn More About the Future of Work?

Get the latest on my website www.carryapaintbrush.com

Unfortunately, as we've gotten pickier, the number of exceptional opportunities has been shrinking. For every job that is posted on job-search websites like Monster.com or CareerBuilder.com, there are thousands of applicants throwing their résumés into the pool.

New college graduates are competing with mid-career professionals who have been laid off, for the few choice jobs that have become available at any given time.

The newbies are seen as young, green, and cheap, but their work ethics, skills, and loyalties are unknowns. The laid-off middle manager has experience and proven skills, but demands more money and may not be willing to work the crazy hours, and keep up with trends like the younger set does.

It's a troublesome time for getting a job. Or should I say, it's a troublesome time for getting a job the *old* way.

So what do we do then? Well, here's what I suggest: we need a new mindset about how we *find and get* work.

Joseph Schumpeter, the famous 20th century economist, adapted and popularized the phrase, "creative destruction" to describe a theory of economic innovation and progress. *"Creative destruction," describes a process in which the old ways of doing things are destroyed and replaced by new ones.*

A great example of this is personal computers. The industry, led by Microsoft and Intel, destroyed the need for mainframe computer companies, but in doing so, created one of the most important inventions of the 20th century.

The old way of getting a job was to read the classifieds or online sites, find a job of interest, and apply. This model is outdated, and doesn't work anymore. So what will "creatively destroy" this outdated model, and what will replace it?

I believe the answers lie in this book. They include:

- A deep knowledge of who and what you want to be in the world.

- A determination to meet and interact with the people who are already doing the kind of work you want to do.

- A creative mindset where you create job opportunities instead of finding job postings.

- A resourcefulness that allows you to critically think about your career and then go after what you want in unconventional ways.

- The ability to reverse engineer the job market and find where you want to work, as opposed to where jobs are open.

- A tenacity that enables you to work smarter than everyone else.

- A uniqueness that differentiates you from the pack and makes employers want YOU.

By applying destructive techniques to your job search, online applications become a thing of the past; the cattle call interview becomes a one-on-one informational session, and waiting for a lucky break becomes the ability to Create Opportunities for

Luck to Happen (which you will learn about in great detail in Chapter 9).

Easy, right? I know it sounds like a lot to manage, but don't worry. I'm going to show you exactly how you can integrate all of these things in your approach to finding a job. You *can* create opportunities to have the career you really want. Read on, dear friend, read on!

Part 2

Define Your Inner Career Artist:
Know Who and What You Want to Be

to be nobody but yourself- in a world which is doing its best, night and day, to make you everybody else - means to fight the hardest battle which any human being can fight, and never stop fighting.

- e. e. cummings

Chapter 4

Define Your Personal Career Brand

To begin, you might be asking, "What the heck is a Personal Career Brand?"

Take a moment and think about what kind of car you drive. Or if you don't drive a car, what kind you would like to drive if you could have one?

What adjectives or characteristics do you associate with your car? Safe? Well-engineered? Versatile? Eco-friendly? Pure driving fun?

Car companies spend gazillions of dollars crafting the brands of the cars they sell. Looking for safety? Buy a Volvo. Superior engineering? Audi. Versatile? How 'bout a Ford minivan? Want to save the planet? You better drive a Toyota Prius. And of course, BMWs want you to know they are the "ultimate driving machine."

When we decide to purchase a car, we consciously or subconsciously have certain attributes in mind that will make the car "feel like me." Outdoorsy types and dog owners love Subarus so much that the company has made dog mats a standard feature for all Subaru models.

Have you ever sat in a car and it just made you feel good? That is exactly the point of the gobs of time and money that the car companies pour into brand development, brand marketing, and advertising.

You are no different.

No, you are not a car. But as you go out and try to "sell" yourself to future employers, it couldn't hurt to know exactly what your own Personal Career Brand (PCB) is, and how you can, like the car companies have done, get people to *buy into your brand.*

Now this isn't as hard as it may seem. Unlike the car companies, you don't need to hire an expensive advertising agency to create clever taglines and ad campaigns. What you do need, however, is to sit yourself down and think about what your brand is, and who you want to be.

Know Who and What You Want to Be

Recently, I coached a client who was stuck in his career search. I had met Erik a few years prior through mutual colleagues, and we became fast friends. Erik had had an amazing career up to that point.

He had started a non-profit in El Salvador, counseled refugees from war-torn countries, worked as a child psychologist, and had run a research and media company that focused on creating programming for children that promoted positive messaging.

Erik was looking for his next adventure when I met him. I had just finished doing a mid-career master's program at the Harvard's Kennedy School of Government and was sharing with him how the program had impacted me.

Erik decided to apply, and after being accepted he spent an amazing ten months on the Harvard campus interacting with 200 like-minded, world-changers as they studied for their masters' degrees. He graduated from the program in May, and by the time we officially started working together, it was November, and he still hadn't found the right "next thing."

Frustrated and losing faith, Erik came to see me and wanted to know if I could help him figure out how he could find work that would truly fulfill him. So I started where I always start with my clients.

I asked, "Who do you want to be in the world?"

Erik was no different than most of the people I've worked with. He had no idea how to answer because no one had ever asked it before. If the first principle of Career Artistry is Claiming Your Career as Your Own, the second is definitely Know Who and What You Want to Be. But how do you figure that out?

My friend and colleague, Alex Kjerulf is an author and speaker on the topic of *Happiness at Work*. Alex is Danish, and if you didn't already know, Denmark has time and again been voted the happiest country in the world. Outsiders who have never experienced Denmark might wonder why. It's dark a lot of the year, and cold. The personal income taxes, at 60 percent, are some of the highest in the Western world, and the cost of living index extremely high. So how is this possible?

I'm sure this pervasive feeling of happiness is comprised of many components. People ride bikes instead of driving, for instance. But I would posit that a large part of their happiness comes from a concept in Danish culture that would puzzle most of us.

Many American companies and organizations *attempt* to create a culture that promotes both *productivity and satisfaction*. But despite these efforts, says Kjerulf, in an op-ed written for the

Christian Science Monitor, the attitude of most U.S. managers is, "You get paid to do your job, not to like it."

As a result, "U.S. workplaces are dominated by status-seeking career climbers, where the paycheck is the only motivator, where employee turnover is shockingly high, where bad management is never challenged, where burnout and cynicism are the order of the day."

In fact, according to a 2010 Conference Board study, Americans of all ages and income brackets continue to grow increasingly unhappy at work. The study goes on to report that only 45 percent of people reported being satisfied or somewhat satisfied with their work, leaving *55 percent either neutral or dissatisfied.* That means that over half of the working population in the U.S. doesn't particularly care for their work.

Denmark, by comparison, reports that 95 percent of their workers are either satisfied or very satisfied at work. What makes the Danes so different from us? It seems that the answer might be very simple. You see, there is a word in Danish, arbejdsglaede (pronounced ah-bites-gleh-the) that literally translates into "happy at work."

Words are born because there is a need to describe something in the particular society that developed them. According to Kjerulf, Danish workplaces have a long-standing tradition of arbejdsglaede, and they want their employees to be happy. In fact, Danes don't just work to get paid; they fully expect to enjoy themselves at work.

The good news is that you don't have to live in Denmark to apply the same concept to your own work culture.

I want you to be happy at work, and one way to ensure that is to make certain that you look for and consider positions that will completely fulfill you. How do you do this? First, you have to discover the place where your Passions, Interests, and Skills intersect. By defining and understanding this sweet spot, you're taking your first steps down the road in creating your Personal Career Brand.

The Intersection of Passions, Interests, and Skills

The first, and probably most important component of your Personal Career Brand, sits at the sweet spot where your Passions, Interests, and Skills overlap.

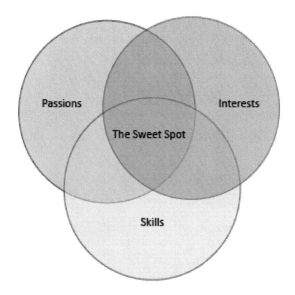

The trick to discovering that sweet spot is to get really clear about what makes you Passionate, what topics never cease to hold your Interest, and what kinds of Skills you possess.

Erik and I sat down one afternoon to find where his Passions, Interests and Skills intersect.

Sitting across the table from him, I laid three plain white sheets of paper between us. At the top of one page, I wrote, "Passions;" on the next I wrote, "Interests," and on the last page, I wrote, "Skills."

"First," I said, "there are no bad ideas in brainstorming. Agreed?"

Erik agreed and I went on.

"We're going to do a little exercise. I want you to verbalize your stream of consciousness. Don't think too hard. Just travel where your thoughts take you."

He nodded and I continued, "I want you to tell me all of the things you are passionate about."

Erik hesitated.

"Passionate? Can you explain what you mean by that?"

"Sure," I said. "**Passions** are things that you crave to do, things you want to work on, and things you want to change. When you're passionate about something, you have boundless enthusiasm, infinite energy, and you never tire from it."

And so he started. Erik's list of Passions contained everything from old architecture to helping underserved populations. He was passionate about animals, introducing people, protecting vulnerable populations, and he even enjoyed video games. He loved organizing, traveling, and making the world a better place.

After he had exhausted his list, I asked, "How did that feel?"

"It felt great. Fantastic, actually. And invigorating. I had forgotten about all those things that really get me going."

"Excellent," I said, reaching for the Interests sheet of paper. "Now let's turn our attention to your Interests."

Interests are topics that keep you engaged and curious. Whether you're fascinated by science or the history of ancient civilizations, when you align your work with things that Interest you, you're bound to stay engaged longer.

And so we went through it again. Erik's Interests spanned from literature to marine biology to diverse cultures and storytelling. The list was long. He had a lot of topics that kept his attention.

Last, we filled out the Skills sheet. **Skills** are things that you have acquired that enable you to do something well. I asked Erik to brag about the things he was good at, and those that others had told him he was good at.

The list was long and full of many interesting things that even in our friendship, I hadn't known about. His list included creating communities, inspiring and motivating people, public speaking, writing, organizing, and research. In making this list, Erik was pleasantly surprised to discover all of the Skills that he had acquired over the years.

"Now," I said to Erik, "we're going to play a game."

I asked him to close his eyes. Then I handed him a felt-tipped pen. Next, I placed his Passions, Interests and Skills pages in front of him. Guiding his hand over the sheets of paper (his eyes were still closed), I asked Erik to place a single dot on each page. He then opened his eyes.

Together, we looked at where the dots had landed.

"Okay," I said, "we're going to brainstorm career ideas for you at the **intersection of your Passions, Interests, and Skills**."

The dot on the **Passions** page was next to "protecting vulnerable populations." The **Interests** dot was next to the word, "culture." Lastly, he had placed a dot next to the **Skill**, "communication."

For the purposes of this round of the game, Erik's task was to brainstorm the types of work that he could do that would allow him to **"protect vulnerable populations within diverse cultures by using his communication skills."**

Here's what he came up with:

Brainstorming Idea #1
Through online and journal articles, videos, and blogs, act as a spokesperson or assembler of spokespeople who address various issues of vulnerable groups to bring awareness to the general public about their challenges.

Brainstorming Idea #2
Get involved in "cause" marketing as it relates to vulnerable populations. Use my communication skills to engage potential donors and sponsors in a cause and then create campaigns to bring awareness of those issues to the general public.

Erik had come up with two great ideas. One idea used his communications skills to bring voice to underserved groups. The second scenario focused on engaging hearts and minds through connection and cause marketing.

Both were very valid paths for Erik to pursue. But we didn't stop there.

Erik closed his eyes again and placed three more dots. They landed on "making the world a better place," "storytelling," and "motivating people."

The following are several ideas that Erik came up with that would allow him to, **"Use storytelling to motivate people to make the world a better place."**

Brainstorming Idea #3
Create educational programming that has meaning for both kids and adults while focusing on collaborative learning and social problem-solving skills. Enable participants to learn about and help solve pressing social issues.

Brainstorming Idea #4
Using video webisodes, create an online show that allows viewers to peer into the lives of people around the globe as they celebrate and struggle with everyday life. Go around the world to see what makes people tick. Show that we have lots in common and many differences to appreciate.

By the end of our working session, Erik, who had been feeling uninspired about his future and was experiencing job-seeker burnout, felt reinvigorated about his prospects.

With this simple exercise, he was able to rediscover what makes him tick and dream up work that would keep him engaged and motivated.

You can do the same.

If you've ever felt stuck or without a specific direction, you can play this game and discover the possibilities that sit at the intersection of your Passions, Interests, and Skills; this realization can be a life changer!

At the end of this chapter, you will have an opportunity to do this exercise for yourself. Play it with a friend or someone you trust. I promise you'll be amazed at what you come up with.

What Kind of Contributor Do You Want to Be?

One of the things that people don't often think about when they're contemplating their working life is the type of Contributor they want to be in their work. This is the second component of your Personal Career Brand.

Before I get into the types of contributors that appear in the workplace, allow me a preface. This is not a personality typing. It is not the Meyers-Briggs test, nor will it help you figure out your overall personality preferences. These styles simply come from my twenty-five years of observation, interaction, and networking. They are tools to help you figure out some of your working style preferences, and in particular, your Contribution Style.

Please be aware that these categories aren't set in stone. I've seen these categories blend and mix frequently. The boundaries between them are quite fluid. In fact, *most of us are either a hybrid of two Contribution Styles*, or *one style that leans toward another style.*

No matter what, these styles are meant to be used as guideposts to help you recognize the types of working opportunities that will truly suit you.

> NOTE: The words *company*, *organization*, and *business* are used interchangeably to indicate an entity with a goal and people employed to achieve that goal. These entities could be for-profit, non-profit, non-governmental organizations (NGO) and public sector.

Now that we've gotten that out of the way, let's get to the nitty-gritty.

The Individual Contributor

Meet Pam. Pam is a connector. She was born with the gift of connecting people. I met Pam soon after I had moved back to Boston. She was aware that I was new in town, and she took it upon herself to make sure that I got connected—to new groups, new friends, and new activities. Over time, Pam and I have become good friends, and I've become part of her inner circle.

At a dinner party where Pam was absent, thirty people went around the room saying how they were connected to the group. Except two, everyone could trace their friendship lineage back to Pam.

In her working life, Pam is at her best when she has a job that allows her to tap into her passion for connecting people. When Pam and I sat down recently to discuss her career, it became clear that she needed to be in an organization where she spent more time looking outward (making connections) than looking inwards (managing or leading people).

When she is meeting people, developing new relationships, and getting them bought-in or onboard, Pam feels empowered and successful. However, when she is called upon to manage people (defining their work, prioritizing their workload, developing their talents) or report to her boss in an organization, Pam feels on edge, challenged, and defensive. Why might this be?

Ultimately, through our discussion, Pam and I discovered that the best kind of role for her in an organization is as an Individual Contributor. An **Individual Contributor** at a company is someone without direct inline responsibility. They are evaluated as individuals, rather than by their contribution as part of a team. They don't have people who report to them, and the people to whom they report usually have given them clear goals, and lots of leeway.

Individual Contributors often have great success in jobs such as sales, business development, research science, and in-house copywriting, as these types of jobs offer independence, quantifiable results, and deliverables.

A challenge for Individual Contributors that I have seen time and again is this: it is often thought that career advancement means being "in charge" of a group. For an Individual Contributor who thrives on working independently, this can be a real challenge.

Imagine a brilliant chemist. This person has been nose-deep in beakers and compounds, and is very content making breakthrough discoveries and the like. During his annual review, our chemist is told that he is making amazing contributions to the company, and they want to reward him with a promotion and a raise. The promotion takes this talented Individual Contributor and puts him in a managerial role.

Suddenly, he is not spending his days with chemicals, but spending time making sure other chemists are doing the right things with their chemicals. In his new role, the chemist becomes frustrated and often bored. He is no longer doing the work that inspires and motivates him. His waning interest leads to a lackluster performance by his team, and the promotion is considered a failure.

Why did this happen? Because you can't change a leopard's spots.

If someone performs at their highest level of productivity and happiness as an Individual Contributor, then that is the role that is best for that person. Yes, a person's Contribution Style can evolve, but it is not something that can be forced.

Forcing someone into a different Contribution Style won't alter how they really *want* to work and interact. It may seem like a form of advancement, but in many cases, it has the opposite results.

So if reading this resonates with you, you might be an Individual Contributor. Look for job types that allow you to work independently on specifically defined tasks. When you do this, you will perform at your peak capacity.

The Team Player

Some people don't work best on their own. They much prefer to be part of a team. **Team Players** are individuals whose Contribution Style is at its peak when they are contributing to a shared objective with their collaborators. Team Players have specific areas of expertise, and they use their expertise to complement the work of the people around them. With Team Players, the whole is definitely greater than the parts.

Think of the difference between a sport like golf and a sport like football. Golf is an individual sport. It's just you, the ball, and the green. The decisions you make are yours and yours alone. Even when you watch the big golf tournaments where they match different countries against one another (like the U.S. and the U.K.), the result of the tournament is the combination of everyone's individual performances.

Football isn't like that. Everyone is playing the game at the same time, and everyone's contributions count at the same time. It's the team strategy and the team execution that determined who wins or loses.

Team players work best on teams, and companies can get the best out of them when they're given shared tasks and shared goals.

If Team Player feels like the right Contribution Style for you, look for companies that work in cross-functional teams so you can focus your energies and talents on fulfilling shared objectives.

The Manager

Managers are people who like to organize, motivate, and give direction to individuals and groups. They're good with planning and the division of labor; they like helping team members overcome obstacles in order to be successful. They are, in general, "people" people.

Many Managers start their careers as individuals contributing to a team, but that is not their fully-realized Contribution Style. What they crave is to be in charge of a group, division, or project. Some want to lead small teams, whereas others desire to be the head of a global practice area. Either way, Managers are at their best when they are at the helm.

Apart from being great organizers and motivators, Managers are the major motivators of productivity within a company. They are both leaders and resources for the teams they manage, and they are great at keeping the team focused on the goals of the project or the organization as a whole. But don't think that the term Manager is in any way rigid or limited.

You'll find Managers throughout the entire infrastructure of an organization. From project managers to team managers, campaign managers to social engagement managers, sales managers to the operating managers, managers exist at every level of an organization.

Meet Beth. Beth is the consummate project manager. She is adept at project planning, great at running and motivating teams, and she's extraordinarily accountable. People love working for Beth, and upper management feels secure with her at the helm.

The funny thing is that Beth doesn't consider herself a project manager. In fact, she doesn't even like managing projects. She just happens to be good at it.

Beth is a graphic designer and would prefer focusing exclusively on the design components of a project, rather than managing the entire team.

However, she is so organized and skilled at management tasks that many of the project management aspects of the job become, by default, her responsibility.

Because of this, Beth often works in a Contribution Style that doesn't feel comfortable to her, and she ends up dissatisfied at work.

It wasn't until Beth was teamed with Jason, a dyed-in-the-wool Manager, that she could comfortably resume her ideal Contribution Style (Team Member) role. From there, it was easier for her to focus on her Passions, Interests, and her preferred Skills; she found happiness at work.

If, like Jason, you truly enjoy organizing people and getting things done, you might be a natural-born Manager. If that's the case, look for jobs where you can put your organizational and people skills to good use. Or join a team and work your way into team management.

The Leader

Many people think that Managers would naturally make good Leaders. Surprisingly, this isn't always the case. Managers are, in general, individuals who can manage projects, people, and tasks to achieve specific results.

Leaders are people who have vision and direction, and the charisma to get people to follow where they lead. If a Manager's job is to make sure that everyone shares the ultimate vision, it's the Leader's job to create that vision.

Leaders have the ability to direct in the current moment, while keeping a keen and visionary eye on the road ahead. They make course corrections, large and small, to stay relevant, on top, or to mobilize change. We all know about famous historical leaders—Abraham Lincoln, Mohandas Gandhi, and Martin Luther King, Jr.

You probably haven't heard of Darwin Smith, but his is an incredible story of great daring and leadership.

I first learned about Smith in Jim Collins's incredible book, *Good to Great*. Collins and his team set out to prove that a company's successful leap from goodness to greatness had *nothing* to do with leadership. In a backward kind of way, they proved their hypothesis right. They found that the leap wasn't about *leadership* as much as it was about a *specific type of leader*—something they went on to dub a *Level 5 leader*.

Darwin Smith was one such leader.

Soon after he became CEO of Kimberly-Clark in 1971, Smith had to face two very difficult truths: 1) Kimberly-Clark, which had been one of the largest producers of paper in the entire country, was "languished in mediocrity," and 2) he had been diagnosed with nose and throat cancer.

After much contemplation about where to take Kimberly-Clark, Smith decided to apply a lesson he had learned from his own cancer experience: "If you have a cancer in your arm, you've got to have the guts to cut off your arm."

Soon thereafter, Smith announced that the company would sell off all of its paper mills.

Analysts derided his decision, and the stock price took a hit. But the move, which one company director called, "the gutsiest decision I've ever seen a CEO make," allowed the company to focus on its paper-based consumer products, buy out rivals, and eventually flourish once again (we've all heard of Kleenex, Scott Tissue and Huggies products, to name a few).

Smith's ability to break from Kimberly-Clark's 100-year history in milling, to envision a different future, and to patiently and courageously lead his company into that future is almost a textbook definition of what it means to be a Leader.

Whether Leaders are leading a company, a non-profit, a government, or a movement, they possess great vision and the charismatic (or in Smith's case, quiet) power to get people to buy in to that vision.

If your talents lie in your ability to move and guide groups, consider looking into careers where you can practice and hone your skills as a Leader.

The Entrepreneur

So far, all of the kinds of Contribution Styles I've discussed exist within a typical workplace. But what types of roles exist outside of the office bubble?

Meet David. David is a start-up guru with more than a half dozen successful companies under his belt. He thrives on coming up with new ideas, testing them against the market, building teams, raising money, and guiding the company into success and increasing its scale. David is an Entrepreneur.

Entrepreneurs are people who have a high tolerance for risk, an insatiable need to build new things, and a contagious energy that people want to be around. Some people are innately entrepreneurial. We all can remember the kid who started his own paper route, or created her own foundation to support a cause.

In general, Entrepreneurs have little tolerance for slow-moving, big-hierarchy companies, which is why they often build their own. Entrepreneurs are capable of wearing multiple hats, thrive under pressure, and require little sleep. Though many

Entrepreneurs build their own companies, a sub-set of Entrepreneurs, referred to as Intrapreneurs, have found ways to be innovative and creative within existing companies.

Social Entrepreneurs are Entrepreneurs who focus their energies on building organizations (both non- and for-profit) that address social and environmental problems and achieve lasting social change.

The interesting thing about many Entrepreneurs is that they're great builders, but not necessarily great maintainers. Because of their inherent risk tolerance and passion for new things, many Entrepreneurs enjoy launching a business, but not the long-term leadership or management of that business.

As a company grows from early stage to later stage, many start-up CEOs step aside and bring in a more managerially-oriented CEO. That person, over time, can then build and lead through the maturation of the company, allowing the Entrepreneur to focus on specific aspects of the business or move onto new things.

If you're the kind of person who sees new opportunities and has the energy and determination to bring new ideas to fruition, you're probably an Entrepreneur. Consider joining a start-up to experience what this type of environment feels like. From there, you can decide if you want to build something on your own.

The Small Business Owner

Small Business Owners are people who run a privately-owned small company. They are similar to Entrepreneurs in that they often start their own businesses, but the biggest difference is in the intended size and scale of the company.

Small businesses tend to be locally owned entities, such as a dry cleaning business, a restaurant, or an accounting practice. Small Business Owners are, in many cases, the "chief cook and bottle washer," and they hire people to support their work and sustain the business.

Small Business Owners have ownership of their business and can create whatever they want, and often act as both manager and leader. They reap the rewards of their successful enterprise but also suffer if it fails.

Although Small Business Owners work for themselves, they do not necessarily enjoy the freedoms that self-employed people (Solo Practitioners, which I will explain next) do, because they carry responsibility for providing enough work to support their employees.

If you have always imagined yourself running your own business, making decisions, managing employees, and seeing the rewards of your own hard work, might consider becoming a Small Business Owner. If you're not in a position to start your own business right now, consider working in a small business where you can see how things operate and get invaluable experience.

The Solo Practitioner

Solo Practitioners are perhaps the most difficult style to define. They are consultants, freelancers, writers, professional speakers, actors, trainers, mediators and a host of other occupations. The thing that Solo Practitioners all have in common is that they work on their own and are not restricted to working for one particular client or company.

Solo Practitioners often have varied income sources and are comfortable always looking for their next gig. They are self-starters and have a healthy tolerance for risk (otherwise they would be somewhere where they could get a regular paycheck).

In general, they thrive in constantly-changing environments and on new assignments, and derive their income from selling their time, their products or their services. Successful Solo Practitioners carefully plan their offerings and construct fee structures that support their financial needs.

Meet Leslie. Leslie is a successful Solo Practioner who works as a personal trainer and wellness coach. She has built her solo-business in a way that affords her the creativity, freedom and flexibility she wants, while enabling her to make a good living.

Leslie makes money in two ways. First, she charges varying fees for the different services she offers. Second, she collects passive income—income that's not dependent on her selling her time, by selling her exercise videos.

If she wanted to grow her business more, Leslie could hire and train new staff, essentially becoming a Small Business Owner. This is a huge step for most independently-minded Solo Practitioners.

If you are a person who wants to be your own boss, and you don't want to hire and manage other people, working as a Solo Practitioner might be right for you. To do this, you need to figure out what kind of goods or services you can offer for sale, and be comfortable not always knowing where your next paycheck is coming from.

Okay, now let's take a breath.

I know that was a lot to take in. But it's important for you to get a taste of the Contribution Styles that are out there, because you need to start thinking about what kind of contributor you'd like to be.

One of the keys to being a successful Career Artist is taking on roles in which you can be successful and fulfilled. If you can find out how you like to contribute, you'll be able to identify suitable roles more easily.

Now that your brain is on "high speed" thinking about your Contribution Style, I want to add another ingredient to your PCB mix—the audience you want to address.

What Size Stage Do You Want to Play On?

As you consider the kind of career you want to create, it's important to figure out what kind of impact you want to have. Do you want to be a big fish in a small pond? A small fish in a big pond? A big fish in a big pond? Understanding the Size of Stage You Want to Play On will help you get clear about the kind of career you want to have.

Meet Isabella. Isabella was a high school junior when I met her, and she was going through the process of deciding where to apply for college. This amazingly mature seventeen-year-old told me that she wanted to "apply to a college that had a gate."

At first I was confused by her statement, until she explained that she wanted a school that felt like a community. She didn't want an urban university where the school buildings were spread about the city, nor was she interested in a sprawling rural campus. She very specifically wanted to be in an environment that was contained, but within easy distance to a city.

What Isabella did in identifying the geographic style of college she wanted to attend was actually much more significant than it appeared at first glance.

Indirectly, she was indicating the size of school she wanted to attend. School size (at the collegiate level) is a really interesting thing to think about. Students can choose from a variety of university and college sizes and styles, and each one provides a different type of experience. Isabella instinctually knew that she was a small, contained school environment where she would have a chance to shine.

In the career world, I call this the *size of the stage*. And in discussing career development with my clients, I often ask them to think about the size of stage they imagine themselves playing on.

Small, Medium, and Large Stages

Some people thrive on the **Small Stage** and prefer to work in small groups, one-on-one, or in a small company. Small Stage players are content with impacting the people around them, and knowing that's where they can be the most effective.

Other people like to play on a **Medium Stage**. This category includes local politicians, business leaders, and community organizers. Medium Stage players like to feel that their contribution has a broader reach than those immediately surrounding them and they like affecting groups and communities.

Bono, the lead singer from U2 plays (literally and figuratively) on the **Big Stage**. As a musician, he is a worldwide sensation. And as a human-rights activist, he works tirelessly to try to eradicate poverty in Africa. Big Stage players want to move hearts and minds across big populations through their actions and words. Politicians and celebrities are natural Big Stage players.

Knowing what type of impact you want to have on the world will really help you with the next part of the development of your Personal Career Brand.

Know What You Want to Get Out of a Job

Who you are, what kind of contributor you want to be, and what stage you want to play on are important, but the picture of your PCB isn't complete until you ask yourself What Do You Want to Get Out of a Job?

Some people live to work and others work to live. Hopefully most of us find a nice midway point that affords us a decent work-life balance. Regardless, knowing what you want to get out of your working life will really help you decide which work opportunities are right for you.

This book is about people, and for people, who are passionate about doing things differently; so if you're reading this book, you aren't a person who works to live.

But what is your relationship to your work? Do you want a career where you get to interact with and meet lots of people? Is that what gives you juice? Or are you looking to make a difference in the world? (This can happen on the Small Stage—

working at a homeless shelter, or on a Big Stage like Bono). Are you looking to discover new things? Make lots of money?

Sometimes we're so focused on "getting" a job that we neglect thinking about *what we want to get from a job.*

Imagine a situation where you're working in an isolation chamber with deadly strains of the influenza virus. If you had told me that what you wanted from your work was *to make scientific breakthroughs*, I'd say this job might be perfect for you. The same is true if you had told me that you wanted to make *a difference in the world* (wouldn't it be great if you could wipe out influenza? You'd be famous!).

But if you told me that one of the things you wanted out of your work was to *interact with and meet people on a regular basis*, I would tell you that a job in the isolation tank was not for you. See what I'm saying?

Understanding what you want to get out of a job is important for another crucial reason—if you don't know what you want, then how do you know when you're not getting it?

In the consulting world, we call this "defining what success looks like." Defining success gives you a baseline to compare things to. The idea is that you can't judge whether a project, campaign, or effort was successful if have no idea what success looks like.

Here's an example. Yvette was a top executive at a company where she had lots of responsibility, tons of decision-making power and a successful product offering. By many peoples' definition, Yvette was a great success, and for a time in her life, she was.

One day, Yvette, a single mom, looked at her life and realized that all of her high-powered success was no longer what she wanted from her work. Instead, she wanted to get off of the high-speed train that was her career and find work that would afford her more flexibility to care for her young daughter.

In other words, *what she wanted to get out of a job had changed*. And although the new job she found came with a lower salary and less responsibility, her gains were enormous.

In order to pick the right type of job, it is really important to know what you want to get out of your working life. Like a painter who envisions and then paints a masterful piece of art, it is your vision of *what you want out of a job* that will lead you to the exact right opportunity.

As you work through the exercises at the end of this chapter, think about your career and what success and fulfillment would look like to you. Without this information, it will be difficult to know when success finds you.

Find Your Special Sauce—Differentiate Yourself from the Pack

The last and perhaps most important part of creating your Personal Career Brand is knowing your Special Sauce. Your Special Sauce is the thing that differentiates you from everyone else out there.

Imagine for a minute that there are two barbecue restaurants, one right across the street from the other. The restaurants are almost completely identical. They both have friendly staff, clean environments, similarly priced good food, and a rack of ribs cooked exactly the way you like them. Yet, Restaurant B always gets more business than Restaurant A. What is it, then, that *differentiates* Restaurant B from Restaurant A?

Well, anyone who knows barbecue knows that the barbecue sauce makes or breaks the ribs. It's the unique ingredients in the *Special Sauce* that makes people choose Restaurant B over A. The same is true of getting work.

In a competitive job market, where you're going head to head with other equally qualified candidates, your Special Sauce is the element that will often become the deciding factor for whether a company chooses you over a thousand other applicants. As such, you have to make sure you know what your Special Sauce is.

Special Sauce takes time to develop, and if you're a Career Starter, you might not have had enough experience or spent enough time to know what yours is. But it is there. I promise. Each of us possesses something unique.

Perhaps it's your sunny disposition that always got you out of detention in high school, or it's your ability to build consensus. Maybe you're great at defusing tense situations with humor.

It's up to you to identify your Special Sauce, and the great thing is that it doesn't have to be strictly limited to your work-life. It could be something about you that people have always admired or found positive. It could be a way of doing things that helps you focus and work hard.

Let me give you an example of what I mean. I've been practicing Kung Fu for a few years now. My trainer, Sifu[2] Yao Li, has an amazing gift. When I first started attending classes, I

---

[2] Sifu is the Chinese word used in Kung Fu to indicate "master" or "teacher."

was quite behind the rest of the group. Every time I came to the studio, Sifu would say, "You're back!" and immediately integrate me into the class. Sifu Yao knew exactly where I was in my learning, whether I was working on forms, boxing, line drills, or even stretching. I felt unique. And special. His attention toward me bonded me to him, to the Kung Fu school, and made me want to attend more frequently.

During my years of training, I've watched as Sifu welcomes new students into the school. Without ever losing track of my progress, he adds this new person to his "mental list." Whether you had been training for a day, a month or a decade, Sifu knew exactly where each student was in their Kung Fu practice.

It turns out that Sifu didn't just make me feel special; he made everyone feel special. This is his Special Sauce, his unique gift. And it's what makes him so loved and his Kung Fu school so successful.

So the question you want to ask yourself is, "What is *my* Special Sauce?" Think about what draws people to you. Or if that isn't working, think about someone you know that people are always drawn to. What makes them unique? And what can you learn from them that would help you nurture your own uniqueness?

Special Sauce is your unspoken brand differentiator. Unlike your skills and experience, your Special Sauce can be the attractor that makes interviewers *want* to hire you.

My Special Sauce is that I can *wrangle* anything. Like a cowboy who herds cattle and brings order to chaos, my gift is that I can wrap my arms around just about any problem and design, strategize, and bring to market, creative solutions.

My Special Sauce has made it possible for me to work with more than fifty organizations in a wide variety of fields and industries, and is proof that in many cases, specific skills aren't the only things that matter. I was hired because they believe that my Special Sauce could help them get things done.

Finding your Special Sauce

Discovering and developing your Special Sauce will help make your story complete. It comes in many flavors and uniquely describes you. Here are some Special Sauce ideas to get your thinking going:

- A gift for getting disagreeing parties to work together.
- A knack for anticipating needs.
- An attention to detail that ensures high quality.
- A compassionate nature that makes people feel comfortable.
- A boldness that motivates and drives people.
- An insatiable curiosity that leads to connections that no one else thought of.
- A patience that allows you to stick with even the most challenging situations.

Take some time to discover what your Special Sauce is. Once you do, you're Personal Career Brand will be complete, and you'll see what a powerful tool it can be.

Chapter 4 Exercises

Create Your Personal Career Brand

Think of your Personal Career Brand (PCB) as a *calling card* that you can "present" to people that you meet along the way as you're discovering and creating your career path.

Plan to spend at least thirty to sixty minutes on this exercise. The resulting list will become the canvas upon which you will paint the career you've always wanted.

Ask a friend, family member, or colleague to help you, or to give you feedback on what you've written. Take your time. Be creative. Think crazy thoughts. Explore. The blank canvas is yours. Have fun filling it!

- **Passions-Interests-Skills exercise**. Grab three sheets of paper and some colored pens. Title one page with Passions, another with Interests, and the third page with Skills. Then start filling them in. Don't be shy. This is your world. Follow the instructions earlier in this chapter and brainstorm your way into a terrific future.

- **Contribution Style exercise**. Review the list of styles in the chapter. Talk to friends and colleagues about your preferences for participating in your work life.

- **Size of Stage exercise**. Think about the type of impact you want to have.

- **What Do You Want to Get Out of a Job? exercise**. What do success and fulfillment at work look like to you? What would make you completely happy at your job? This list is how you think about what success looks like.

- **Your Special Sauce exercise**. Think about your personal pizzazz. What makes you unique and compelling? Playing to this strength can really help.

- **Brainstorm Idea exercise**: Take all that you've learned about yourself and brainstorm fun and fascinating ideas for your work life.

As a Career Artist, my PCB is always growing, evolving, and morphing. Below is what my PCB looked like before I decided to write this book. Use it as an example, and have fun creating your own!

Susanne's PCB

- **Passions:** storytelling, creating new things, teaching, helping people
- **Interests:** human condition, career development, making the world a better place
- **Skills:** coaching, writing, public speaking, website design and development
- **Contribution Style:** Individual Contributor, Leader
- **Size of Stage:** National, big impact
- **What Do I Want to Get Out of the Job?:** Become a best-selling author and speaker
- **Special Sauce:** My ability to motivate people to envision what they can become
- **Brainstorm Idea:** Use my writing and coaching skills to share stories, techniques and tools, and help readers create the career they've always wanted

---

Chapter 5

Get a Mentor

A big part of who you are as a person is shaped by the people who teach you. The same goes for who you are as a Career Artist. Whether for life or for work, tons of literature has been written about the importance of having a Mentor. Whether your Mentor is inside or outside your work environment, the value of a good Mentor is immeasurable. Ask any successful person and chances are high that they'll tell you that they've had at least one Mentor in their life.

Mentors provide essential guidance and coaching as your career develops. They can help with building and maintaining your career network and help you celebrate job successes as well as talk you through job challenges. From encouragement to providing a mirror for self-examination and growth, having a committed Mentor in your life can make your career development infinitely easier.

My mentor's name is David. He's 84, and the reason I am writing this book. David didn't become my Mentor and friend until well into my career life. Introduced by a family member, our mentor-mentee relationship is a perfect match. He delights in my successes and holds my hand through difficult times. He provides keen counsel, challenges my assumptions, and encourages me to move past my own fears.

Like me, he is sensitive and a good reader of people. He hasn't had one singular career (quite unique for his generation) and believes that I can be anything I want to be.

In fact, it was after he attended a speech that I gave at Brandeis University about career development that he suggested I write this book. Without him in my life, you wouldn't be reading these words right now. Which in and of itself should indicate to you the immensely important role a Mentor can play in your life.

To find a Mentor, you may need to step out of your comfort zone. I know this can be scary. But believe me when I tell you that *people love to help other people*. It's in our nature. If you can get up the gumption to approach potential Mentors and explain to them what you're looking for, you'll be surprised at the positive reactions you'll get.

You might find your Mentor at work, through family members, friends, or at the random July 4th picnic. You might start by asking someone you think might be a good fit to have lunch with you, where you can ask for their advice on a specific topic. You could follow up with a second meeting during which you would report on your progress and see if they're taking a special interest in you.

In time, you'll get a sense of whether or not this person is interested in filling this incredibly important role in your life. And if you pick the right Mentor (or Mentors, in fact), they'll get as much out of the relationship as you do.

Mentoring allows the Mentor to act as a sage advisor. But more importantly, as David tells me all the time, it fulfills a need that all human beings have—to feel needed. I need David, and it turns out that my needing him makes him feel needed, youthful, invigorated, and engaged. I don't believe him. I think he feels youthful and invigorated because, at 84, he still plays hard-core tennis three times a week. But I do know that he gets a lot from our relationship, and I encourage you to go out and find your own David. I promise you that it can make all the difference in the world.

Chapter 6

Communicate Like a Pro: The End of Um, Ah and OMG

Before I get into restoring normalcy in communication, let me just get this out of the way right up front. I'm about to sound like an old fogie. I know that every generation feels that the next generation is doomed. Letter writers blame typewriters for the demise of handwritten correspondence. Letter typers blame computers and email for the end of long, thoughtful communication. And I blame texting and Twitter for destroying our ability to write a complete sentence—no matter your age.

Meet Dave. Dave had just graduated from college when I began working with him. He was eager and personable, but a terrible communicator. Well, terrible by my standards. He had somehow managed to make it through college without learning how to communicate like a responsible adult.

Dave didn't know how to confirm an appointment, didn't know how to write an email, and he didn't realize that texting me, like he did with his friends, was not an appropriate means of conducting our professional relationship.

Most importantly, he didn't know how to have a conversation with me. Dave needed guidance to help him learn how to communicate in the *professional* world.

What I realized is that he didn't know how to organize his thoughts when it came to thinking in a professional manner.

Though he had successfully written all sorts of academic papers and had participated effectively in the classroom, Dave was lacking in his ability to drive a conversation or tell a coherent story.

Storytelling is an essential part of communication. In Chapter 17, you will have an opportunity to take out your Paintbrush and Paint your own stories, but for our purposes here, we're going to use a few of the concepts of storytelling to learn how to create solid conversations and to write powerful communiqués.

The lesson we can learn from great storytelling is that every communication—written, verbal, phone, or in person—must have a beginning, a middle and an end, better known as a 3-Act Structure.

Mastery of storytelling frameworks can make even the most daunting conversations go smoothly. By knowing where to start (Act 1), what you want to talk about (Act 2), and where you want to end up (Act 3), you'll gain control over your ability to communicate.

Let's break this down a bit more by using the example of getting a Mentor from the previous chapter.

Uncle Mike is a successful and respected businessman. He has always been your "fun uncle," but now you would like the relationship to be something more. You want to ask him to consider becoming your Mentor. How do you do this?

Walking up to him at the next family gathering and saying, "Uncle Mike, will you be my mentor?" might get him to say "Yes," but it's not the most compelling way to get his attention, or to have him take you seriously. Besides, he'll have no idea what type of mentoring you are seeking.

Instead, pull him aside at the next family gathering and Communicate with him Like a Pro.

Act 1—The Starting Point (Set-up)

> *"Uncle Mike, as you know I'm just graduating from college (or thinking about a career transition; whatever your particular circumstance) and I've been really considering my career options.*

Act 2—The Discussion Point (Purpose)

> *"You've always been my fun, cool uncle, but I also know that you're a successful businessman and community leader."*

Act 3—The Ending Point (The "Ask")

> *"I was wondering if you'd be willing to sit down with me and talk about my future. I would really welcome any advice you'd have for me and would be happy to come to your office at your convenience."*

Can you imagine how this approach would generate a different response from Uncle Mike? Because you approached him in a serious, professional way, he will take you seriously. By explaining: 1) your current situation, 2) your reason for approaching him, and 3) your "ask," you have demonstrated that you are genuine in your request. Chances are high that he'll not only make time to meet with you, but he'll start to take an interest in you.

Learning how to communicate in full thoughts takes practice. If you can continually remind yourself, even in conversations that are happening on the fly, that every story has a beginning, middle, and end, I guarantee that people will begin to respond to you differently.

If you learn only one thing from this book, make it this one.

The End of Um, Ah, and OMG

Remember when I said I blame text and Twitter for destroying our ability to write a complete sentence? Get ready for this one.

For some time now, I've heard horror stories about hiring managers receiving résumés and cover letters from applicants with text-isms (OMG, ENUF, GR8, and ☺) and other jargony language. I thought they were just urban legends and dispelled them as tall tales—until I had experienced it for myself.

I thought I had done a good job working with Dave. We were at the point where he could direct each of our meetings with very little input from me. His weekly updates were complete and well organized. And we had connected on instant messenger (IM) so we could make use of phone, email, and IM to most effectively conduct our business together. It turned out that IM was a fatal flaw, and I found it out the hard way.

The time had arrived for Dave to begin growing his career network (you will learn how to do this in Chapter 12: Network by 5s). He had done his homework, as outlined in this book, and was ready to start meeting people who could help his career take off.

As chance would have it, the CEO of the non-profit Dave was most interested in was a friend and colleague of mine. Though it is traditionally not my practice, I agreed to reach out to my friend Brian, to see if he'd be willing to meet with Dave and talk with him about his organization.

I composed something similar to the following email:

Dear Brian:

I hope this note finds you doing well.

When I spent the National Service Day volunteering at Organization X, I bonded with one of your exceptional program graduates, Jane Frankln. What an outstanding young woman she is! She is smart, clear, polite and mature beyond her years. Jane and I have stayed in touch via email and she told me she got accepted into her first choice college. It's all very exciting and what you are doing with these kids to help them get ready for higher education is simply amazing. Congratulations.

I'm writing to you today on behalf of a young mentee of mine named Dave Smith (copied on this email). Dave just graduated from college with a degree in psychology, and he is looking to find a job working with kids in a teaching environment. He has become quite familiar with Organization X, and I know that he is incredibly enthusiastic about the possibility of joining your team.

I was wondering if you, or someone else at Organization X, would be willing to take a few minutes to speak with Dave. As a recent graduate, I believe that he could be a real asset to the company and think you would really enjoy meeting him. I wholeheartedly support his candidacy.

I will take the bold step of asking Dave to follow up with you directly. Thanks in advance for your consideration.

Best Regards,

Susanne Goldstein

While composing this email, I had an IM window open and was having a side discussion with Dave. I wrote him that I was in the process of composing an introductory email to Brian. I told him I had copied him on the email. And in IM, I said to him,

> *You will notice at the end of the email, I have given him an indication that you will follow up first. This is your responsibility, not his. When you receive the email, you should click "Reply All" so that I am copied & then write something like – Susanne thank for the intron and Brian nice to virtually meet you. I am enthusiastic to learn more about the company...*

IM is an imperfect form of communication. We tend to write quickly and in short bursts. Accuracy gives way to getting to the point quickly and this is where I made my mistake. I assumed that Dave was ready to Communicate Like a Pro.

About five minutes after my email had been sent, I received Dave's email reply. It said:

> *Susanne thank for the intron and Brian nice to virtually meet you. I am enthusiastic to learn more about the company...*

He had taken my IM to him, typos, unfinished sentences and all, and *copied and pasted it into a reply email to the person he wanted to hire him.*

I was furious. Within a millisecond, I had Dave on the phone.

"What were you thinking?" I said, not trying to hide my irritation.

He was baffled. "I did what you told me to do," he replied in his own defense.

I asked Dave to open up the email he had sent and read it to me out loud. He did.

"Would you hire that person?" I asked.

"No," he confessed.

"Why is that?"

I could almost hear Dave's face contorting through the phone once he realized his mistakes. That's when two things occurred to me: 1) In the 140-character world of texting, Facebook, Twitter and the like, people have forgotten how to write full sentences, and 2) Within this 140-character world, speed is more important than accuracy. That's why no one spends the time to re-read their own writing, or to double-check to make sure what they have written is what they actually intended to say.

You can imagine how I felt when Dave took my half-baked, typo-ridden IM message and pasted it, unchecked, into an email and sent it to a potential employer.

Folks, this simply will not do. We all need to up our game and communicate more professionally. Not just the young 140-character set, but all of us. Here are several things you need to know if you want to Communicate Like a Pro.

1) Unless you are typing your status in Facebook, texting, or emailing with your personal friends, it is NEVER OKAY to use text-isms.

2) Consider every person you meet as someone who could potentially advance your career. Speaking with respect and without gimmick will put many more people in your corner.

3) Think before you speak. Listen before you think.

4) Make sure that when you have something to say, you think about what you want to convey. Use a 3-Act structure to help you get there.

5) Be open and ready to engage in mature dialog.

6) If you are re-using the text from one email to send to a different recipient, you better make sure that the name, company information and any other personalization has been updated appropriately.

7) Re-read every email, note, and letter you write at least three times (see The Rule of 3Cs that follows to learn more about this).

8) It is okay to say you don't know something. Asking questions shows curiosity and intelligence, which is good.

Now it's very easy for me to sit here and give you a bunch of general tips on how to communicate more effectively. For some of you, I'm hoping this stuff is old hat. But just in case it isn't, I'm going to put my money where my mouth is, and show you how to strengthen your communication skills with the most common form of business communication we have today—email.

Writing a Great Email

Of the hundreds of emails I receive each day, only a handful are well-conceived and well-written. Writing a good email is a Skill that you must perfect if you want to be a successful Career Artist, and the good news is that it isn't rocket science.

However, it does take time.

I usually give myself about twenty minutes to compose a really good email. At the beginning, you should plan on giving yourself more time. Remember, what you write in this email says an awful lot about you, and you want to make sure that you're completely in control of how your words can be interpreted.

To learn more about this, let's take a look at the email I wrote introducing Dave to Brian and review how I used the 3-Act structure to get my message across.

Act 1—The Starting Point (Set-Up)

> *When I spent the National Service Day volunteering at Organization X, I bonded with one of your exceptional program graduates, Jane Franklin. What an outstanding young woman she is! She is smart, clear, polite and mature beyond her years. Jane and I have stayed in touch via email and she told me she got accepted into her first choice college. It's all very exciting and what you are doing with these kids to help them get ready for higher education is simply amazing. Congratulations.*

In the opening of you email, you should establish a point of connection with your recipient. Doing this allows you to create an atmosphere of reciprocity and your reader will be more open to any request you might have.

Act 2—The Discussion Point (Purpose)

I'm writing to you today on behalf of a young mentee of mine named Dave Smith (copied on this email). Dave just graduated from college with a degree in psychology and he is looking to find a job working with kids in a teaching environment. He has become quite familiar with Organization X, and I know that he is incredibly enthusiastic about the possibility of joining your team

The point of the second act is to introduce the purpose of your email in a cohesive and compact way. The technique here is that you want to give enough information to pique your reader's interest, but not so much that you're belaboring the point.

Act 3—The Ending Point (The "Ask")

I was wondering if you, or someone else at Organization X, would be willing to take a few minutes to meet with Dave. As a recent graduate, I believe that he could be a real asset to the company and think you would really enjoy meeting him. I wholeheartedly support his candidacy.

I will take the bold step of asking Dave to follow up with you directly. Thanks in advance for your consideration.

In the third act, you want to make the "ask" of your reader. An "ask" is the specific request that you're making. It should be simple and clear, and something that the reader can actually deliver on. Be careful to make sure that your "ask" is not outside the realm of the feasible. It won't help you in your quest, and it's most likely that your email will end up in the Deleted folder.

Conclude by proposing a "next step." Make it clear whose court the ball is in and who is responsible for the next action step.

The Rule of 3Cs

Now sit back from your computer and prepare yourself to re-read your email three times. Never, ever hit "Send" on an email until you have applied the Rule of 3Cs.

The first "C" stands for context. The context review allows you to make sure that you have appropriately set the stage for your reader. Ask yourself, "Does each paragraph as a whole convey your desired point?" and "Do the paragraphs make sense as a progression?"

The second "C" is for content. Knowing what each paragraph is supposed to convey, are you using the best words to convey it? Look at each word critically. If you need a better word, find one. Don't use big words for the sake of using big words. Choose the *right* words.

The third "C" is for copy editing. Read each word carefully looking for typos and incorrect grammar. Don't rely on the spell checker in your email program; it doesn't correct words that you've used incorrectly. For instance, my fingers constantly type the word "you" when I mean "your" and vice versa. A spell checker won't catch that.

And please re-learn when to use "your" versus "you're." If there's one grammatical error I see over and over again, it's this one.

Once you have completed the Rule of 3Cs, decide on the appropriate salutations for the beginning and end of your email, write a clear subject heading, and make sure you're using the correct recipient name and email address.

Your Last Name Matters

Last, but definitely not least, learn to love your last name. Whether you are introducing yourself at the beginning of the email, signing off at the end of your email, (or meeting someone in person for that matter) it's time for you to start using your last name.

Stating your last name is a lost art form, and one that I think deserves reviving. Introducing yourself by your first name only is too casual in a business environment and does nothing to help people remember you. By owning both your first AND last names, you're saying, "This is who I am, and I'm ready for business." It's a sign that you're capable of introducing yourself to anyone, be it a co-worker, a hiring manager, or a CEO. If you don't believe me, pay attention next time you're in a group of professional people. You'll start to notice the power in which some people own their last name.

So type your first and last name at the end of your email, and hit "Send."

You've now learned how to Communicate Like a Pro.

Chapter 6 Exercises

Write a Great Email

You're not going to believe how many doors a great email will open until you start writing them. This takes practice and a change in behavior.

I've discovered that the best way to develop a new skill or habit is to think about that behavior as a "theme" for one entire week.

Years ago, I noticed that the house was getting messy more often than I wanted. So I decided that for one entire week, my theme would be, "the week of putting things away."

Every day for one week, whatever I touched I put back where it belonged when I was done with it. At the end of the week, I was amazed at how great the house looked, and I didn't have to set aside time on the weekend just to clean up.

By taking that extra millisecond to do something differently, I had created a new good habit. It saved me time then, and it continues to save me time now, many years later.

I want you to become a great writer of emails. And if you make "writing a great email" your theme for an entire week, something tells me you'll be pretty happy with the results.

When you're writing emails this week, even if it's just to a friend about dinner plans, here's what I want you to do:

- Implement a 3-Act structure that contains one or two sentences in three separate paragraphs that explain your:

- Starting Point (Set-Up)
- Discussion Point (Purpose)
- Ending Point (The "Ask")

Before you hit "Send" on any email, make sure you run it through the Rule of 3Cs.

Sure, your friends and family might think you've gone a little cuckoo, but there really is no better way to practice writing a good email than to write a lot of emails.

After you've lived with this theme for seven days, review the emails in your "Sent" folder. They should appear to have a stronger writing style, and you should notice that your communications are clear and easier to understand than the emails you wrote before doing this exercise.

Once this method of email writing has become a habit, you'll be ready to move on and write emails to the people who are going to help your career move forward.

Stop Using Um, Ah, and OMG

Have you ever gotten a new car and suddenly noticed that everyone on the road seemed to be driving the same make or model? Of course, this isn't true, but it's our perception. And that's because what we focus on expands to fill our consciousness.

So here's what I want you to do to become more aware of how often you use certain phrases that might make you appear less than "all that." The next time you're on a subway, bus, at work, in a restaurant, or anywhere in public, listen carefully to how people are speaking.

Pick a phrase like, "you know," and notice how many times in one given day you hear people overusing that phrase. By focusing your attention on that expression, and that expression only, you will become aware of how often others use it, and how often you use it as well.

Every day for the next two weeks, choose one word or phrase that you'll focus on and listen for; choose phrases such as, "um," "ah," "like," and "oh my god."

After completing this exercise each day, ask yourself which word habits you have that you'd like to delete from your vocabulary. You'll be amazed at how your speech patterns change.

This is a great exercise to do before you meet with someone that can be a big influence on the direction of your career.

Chapter 7

Get Your Résumé & References in Order

This book focuses on knowing who you are and getting you in front of people who can help move your career forward. As convincing as you may be in person, you will need to have a series of documents to support your candidacy.

Create a Killer Résumé

Writing a good résumé is hard. There, I said it. Sure, you can look online, find a template, fill in all of the appropriate boxes and have a résumé. But does that sheet of paper (or electronic file) really represent you?

Writing a killer résumé that represents the real you, makes you stand out from the crowd and gives a sense of you as a real person, is another really important skill for you to learn. Unfortunately, that's really hard, and it's not what this book is about.

But you will need a good résumé. I suggest you use all of the resources at your disposal to craft something interesting and unique that speaks to who you are, and makes you stand out from the crowd.

You can also visit my website www.carryapaintbrush.com to get some hints on successful résumé writing.

Get Your References in Order

Beside your résumé, you'll need to get a reference sheet in order. A reference sheet consists of a list of people who are willing to talk to an interviewer on your behalf. Choosing the right people to be *a reference* for you is critical.

Many interviewers, as part of their due diligence call upon your references to confirm that the things you've said about yourself are true, and find out more about your work and character.

So it's important that you select people you trust who can speak positively about your experience, skills, collaborative nature, personality, and performance.

If you don't have any supportive work references, you might ask for a *character reference* from someone at your school, a volunteer activity, a sports team, or a religious organization.

And before putting someone's name, title, company, relationship (i.e., I reported to him) and contact information on your reference sheet, get their permission. Some people might not want to act as reference, so it's your job to make sure that they agree before you include them.

Bring your reference sheet to your interview with your résumé, and do your reference people a favor by giving them a "heads up" when phone calls or email might be coming their way.

Again, check out my website www.carryapaintbrush.com to get links to some good resources.

Chapter 8

Grab Your Paintbrush and Get Going

I want you to take a deep breath. Because in the last seven chapters you have kicked off a journey that is going to forever change the way you look at your working life.

You've Claimed Your Career as Your Own, developed a Personal Career Brand and identified your Special Sauce.

You've found a great Mentor, learned to Communicate Like a Pro and can now write brilliant and effective emails.

Your résumé and references are in order, and now it is time to get going.

So grab your Paintbrush and let's start Painting the future you've always dream of.

.

Part 3

Art Direct Your Own Career: Paint Doors and Create Opportunities for Luck to Happen

I'm a great believer in luck and I find the harder I work, the more I have of it.

- Thomas Jefferson

Chapter 9

Carry a Paintbrush

Many successful people attribute their success to "good luck." Let me share a secret with you. Luck doesn't just happen. Yes, I suppose if you play the lottery and your number comes up, that could be considered luck (I would actually consider it probability). But the business people, politicians, entertainers, and others who claim luck as the primary reason for their achievements aren't really telling you the whole story.

Luck Doesn't Just Happen

Although luck doesn't just happen, it can be nudged, nurtured, and encouraged into existence. I call this process Painting Doors and Creating Opportunities for Luck to Happen.

When I was twenty-three years old, I had the great honor of working as an assistant for John Schlesinger, the Academy Award winning film director. When I landed that job, I thought, "I'm the luckiest girl in the world." But like I said, that's not telling the whole story. This is.

After I completed my semester abroad in London, I returned to Ithaca to complete my studies at Cornell.

But I was dying inside. I missed London and my boss, Jason, from the National Theatre. I missed being around the creative process on a daily basis, and I couldn't stand living away from my then-boyfriend for one minute longer. And I was graduating, which meant that it was time to truly get serious about my career.

As I told you, I had already bucked the system and skipped the on-campus interviews for engineering jobs. The only thing I was sure of at the time was that I wanted to make movies, and I wanted to go back to London. In my mind, neither of those were options; they were absolute requirements. I had to find a way to make it happen. But how?

It is at these moments, when your Bucket of Paint and Paintbrush are going to come in really handy.

Creating Opportunities for Luck to Happen

If luck doesn't just happen, how do you get lucky things to happen? There is really only one answer: creative hard work. What does that mean? It means you have to be creative about how you approach getting what you want, and then you must work hard to get it. If you don't believe me yet, you will when I finish the story of how I got back to London.

I remember driving home to Boston after graduation. With a U-haul trailer in tow, I was full of sadness that college was over, and I was equally full of excitement about my future. In my mind, my life was beginning to spell itself out. I was going to make movies, live in Europe, and pursue my "happily ever after."

Unfortunately, I was, once again, starting from scratch. I didn't have a job, didn't know anyone in the London film community, and didn't have any industry connections at all.

At my local library (remember, this was before the Internet, before email, and before big online databases), I found a booked called *Film Directors* that listed hundreds of movie directors from the U.S., UK, and other countries. Each entry contained a snail-mail address, a phone number, and a listing of each director's body of work.

Every day, for weeks, I sat in my attic bedroom with my Mac 128k computer dreaming up ways that I could make contact with these directors.

At first, I thought I could send them a cover letter and résumé, but I was afraid that would just get filed away with other letters of that sort. Next, I considered sending a video of my student film, but was concerned that my film wouldn't duly impress them. And then it occurred to me. I decided to appeal to their human side, and tell them the truth.

Using the Film Directors book as my guide, I identified every director who lived in London, and made notes on what movies they had done that I had seen. I also made a list to take to the video store to rent the movies I wanted to see.

One by one, I went down the list and wrote each director a *personal letter*. In each letter, I introduced myself and told how I had previously worked at the National Theatre and how much I appreciated that the British government supported national arts programs. I told them I admired their work and mentioned a *particular part of a specific movie* that I thought was profound, or interesting, or beautiful.

Next, I told them I was interested in breaking into the film business, and would welcome the opportunity to meet with them. I explained that I would be in London for a wedding from this date to that date, and I'd be grateful if they would consider meeting with me.

I worked hard. I did my research and watched a lot of movies all in a very compressed time period. I used a mail-merge program on my Mac to *create letters with a personalized greeting, pertinent movie references, and context.* I provided both my U.S. and UK contact information. By the middle of June, I had mailed more than fifty letters.

In early July, I was getting ready to head to London for my friend's wedding and hadn't yet received any positive responses. I had received a few kindly handwritten "no thank you" letters, but nothing that gave me hope. When I boarded the plane to fly across the Atlantic, I didn't have a single meeting set up. I tried not to feel dejected.

When I got to London, I got so engrossed in wedding planning that I completely forgot about my job worries. One afternoon I returned to the house and found a message from John Schlesinger himself. I couldn't believe my luck. I immediately called back.

"Mr. Schlesinger is staffing up a new movie," his secretary told me. "He's very interested in meeting with you."

Are you kidding? John Schlesinger wanted to meet with me?

I went to John's home office the following day, barely able to breathe through my excitement and anxiety. If you don't know his work (you should), he won the Academy Award for *Midnight Cowboy* and directed the critically acclaimed movies like *Marathon Man* and *Sunday Bloody Sunday*.

The movie John was about to make was called *Madame Sousatzka* and it was to star Shirley MacLaine as a brilliant instructor of classical pianists. John was looking for an assistant and directing trainee for the film.

As his *director's assistant* I would act as his eyes and ears and provide a shield against the constant barrage of questions and issues that come before a director during a shoot. A good personality fit was essential in this scenario and John and I sat down to get to know each other.

We spoke of my experience in film school, my time at the National Theatre, and my desire to get real industry experience. He told me how much he appreciated my letter and how my personal interest in one of his movies made him select my résumé from the pile.

We discovered a shared love of classical piano, and I told him that I had been classically trained since the age of four. Within an hour of meeting, I found myself sitting at his piano playing Beethoven's Moonlight Sonata for him.

John hired me on the spot.

See, it wasn't just getting lucky. In doing all of the work needed to meet people in the field in which I wanted to work, I had Created an Opportunity for Luck to Happen.

My point is that there is much more you can do besides applying for jobs online. You can Create Opportunities for yourself at any time you want. And this is where your Paintbrush comes in.

Imagine for a minute that you're in a white room. It's cube-shaped and 12 x 12 feet in size, and there is no door, no window, no ventilation shaft, nothing. The only things with you in the room are a Bucket of Paint and a Paintbrush. Your task is to get out of the room. What do you do?

I assume, since you have been reading this book, you actually know where I am going here. Pick up the Paintbrush, dip it in the Bucket of Paint, Paint a Door on the wall, Open the Door and walk out. Right? This is exactly how I want you to think about getting the kind of job you've always wanted. But instead of Painting a Door to get "out" of the room, I want you to Paint a Door that gets you "into" the job.

Finding Your Paintbrush

So how did I land my dream job with one of the most important directors in the entire film industry? It's really quite simple; I used my Paintbrush, and here's what that means.

Think of your Paintbrush as your instrument for creatively figuring out how to tackle any situation, solve any problem, and meet anyone. A Paintbrush is generally thought of as an artist's tool, but I disagree. In fact, I believe I discovered how to use mine when I was in engineering school, and I'd like to share that experience to help you.

Engineers use a very simple framework for understanding and then solving problems called an "If, then" statement. "If, then" statements provide a framework for breaking problems into digestible parts, and context for devising solutions. By understanding what you want to achieve, (the "If" part of the statement), you can define action steps (the "then" part of the statement) to get you there. Here are some examples:

- "**If** you want to take an afternoon drive, **then** you should bring keys to start the car."

- "**If** you want to get good grades on a test, **then** you should study hard."

- "**If** you want to lose weight, **then** you should stop eating candy."

In my example above, my "If, then" would go something like this:

*"**If** I want to work in the film industry in London, **then** I better figure out how to meet people who are already working in the film industry in London, and then get them to help me."*

My "If, then" statement helped me break down the problem and the solution I devised—writing to directors, was clear and actionable.

With each letter, I had Painted a Door and Created an Opportunity for Luck to Happen. All I needed the directors to do now, was invite me in.

You, too, can create these doorways, and it is not nearly as scary as it may seem. Just by being exposed to the concept of Carrying a Paintbrush, your orientation toward problem-solving will change. At first, you might not feel like you have the creativity, guts, or inspiration for this new way of looking at the world.

But give it some time. We're talking about changing some life-long embedded habits. Just remember, when you finally decide to embrace your Paintbrush, the world will become your canvas.

By defining yourself, and creatively working hard, you will be able to paint doorways into meeting the people, organizations and opportunities you've always dreamed about, and keep them open for a long time. Sure, we all need a little "luck." But just like my opportunity with John Schlesinger, you don't have to wait for luck; you can actually make it happen.

Chapter 9 Exercises

Creating "If, Then" Statements

If you ever feel like a task is insurmountable, "If, then" statements are for you. By breaking down a problem and understanding what you want to achieve, (the "If" part of the statement), you can define action steps (the "then" part of the statement) to get you there.

Now it's your turn to grab your Paintbrush and Create Opportunities for yourself. "If, then" statements are a great way to get started.

- Grab a piece of paper and start by writing down the "If" you want to bring about.

- Make a list of all of the things that could make that "If" happen. The things on your list are the "thens."

- Next, combine your "Ifs" with the various "thens" in the form of:

  "If I want [insert a description of what you want], then I need to [insert a description of what you need to do to make the "If" possible].

Sometimes it might take a few steps in series to get you from the place you are now, to the place you want to be. So consider daisy-chaining some "If, thens" together to create the outcomes you want.

Remember, you are the owner of your own career, and "If, then" statements are a great way of helping you know where to step next.

Chapter 10

Reverse Engineer the Job Market

Carrying a Paintbrush is the first step in Creating Opportunities for Luck to Happen. The second is a technique I call *Reverse Engineering the Job Market.*

Reverse Engineering is a term that simply means taking something apart so you understand how it was built. It is often thought of as *going backward through the development cycle.*

A traditional job search involves finding lists of job openings and then deciding which ones are a good fit for you. In this model, you are always trying to fit yourself into the mold of the job description.

Reverse Engineering the Marketing turns this model on its head. Instead of looking for jobs and trying to fit yourself into them, you look for the kinds of places you want to work and types of people you want to work with, and work your way into them.

The basic idea here is that it's incredibly difficult to find a job opening that is at a company you like, in a place you want to live, that pays you an appropriate wage and also aligns with your Passions, your Interests and your Skills.

What if, instead, you searched out companies where you *knew* you'd be a good fit? And what then, if you could use your Paintbrush to meet people within these companies to connect with and Create Opportunities for Luck to Happen?

Reverse Engineering the Job Marketing is a completely different way of going about finding work, and it is an essential component of being the Artistic Director of Your Own Career.

Now, you might be saying to yourself, "I have no idea how to do this!"

Don't worry. **Reverse Engineering works for Career Starters, Career Transitioners and even Solo Practitioners.** It is a major technique that I have used to build a large part of my career. And it can work for you too.

If you've done the exercises in the previous chapters, you are well prepared for this next step. And even if you haven't, read on.

You're going to meet two people: Trey, a Career Starter, and George, a mid-Career Transitioner. In both of their stories, you'll see how easy it is to find companies and organizations that are doing things that get you really excited.

Meet Trey. Trey was graduating from college and had no idea how to go about finding a job when his parents introduced him to me. Trey is a smart guy. He has really good instincts and is a charming and articulate person. However, Trey's offline potential wasn't translating to the online world, where most people apply for jobs. Additionally, he didn't really know what kind of job he wanted, nor the kinds of organization he wanted to work for.

After working on his Personal Career Brand (like you hopefully did in Chapter 4) Trey determined that he wanted to find a job where he could "use his leadership and communication skills to help inner city kids have a better chance in the future."

He then wrote an "If, then" statement to help him achieve his PCB goal. It looked like this:

"If I want to help inner city kids have a chance in the future, then I need first need to find out what organizations are already working with kids in the inner city."

Now, as you might imagine, there are a lot of organizations and companies working in this area, and many ways for Trey to get involved. From prevention programs to social services and afterschool activities, from non-profits, to public school systems to private education companies, the question became, how could Trey find out *what organizations were already* doing this kind of work?

So I sent him on a search. His assignment was this: *find places you want to work.* Don't worry if a job exists or if you think you're qualified. Just identify companies and organizations that are already doing exactly the kinds of things you want to be doing.

The problem was that Trey had no idea how to do this, and I don't blame him. This isn't something that college career service offices prepare students to do (this is an unfortunate fact, but I'll save that for another book!)

So I gave Trey a few guidelines about how to get started, how to conduct his search, how to keep track of his findings, and where to look.

First, we set up a spreadsheet where he could capture details of companies as he found them. (I'm a big fan of Google Docs, which provides free web-based applications that work in a similar manner as today's popular productivity applications like Microsoft Excel and Word).

Second, we labeled the columns of the spreadsheet:

- Name of company.
- What they do.
- Why I'm excited about them.
- What I can imagine doing if I worked there.
- The URL (website address).
- How I found them.

Third, I guided him to one of my favorite websites, Volunteer Match (www.volunteermatch.com). Volunteer Match (VM) is a fantastic site where volunteers are matched with volunteer opportunities. In fact, 75,000 non-profit organizations use Volunteer Match as their preferred Internet recruiting tool.

I told Trey I wanted him to use VM to find out what kinds of organizations were doing work with inner city kids. And although most people visit VM to find out where they can volunteer or do community service, I didn't want Trey to use VM this way.

I wanted him to Reverse Engineer VM and use it as a *resource* for finding out which non-profits were doing what.

What was great, is that Trey didn't feel any pressure for finding the right "job match." Instead of reading job listings, he focused on company and organization profiles to find which ones ran programs or provided products and services that were of interest to him.

By doing this, he was finding places to work that would help him reach his goal of working with inner city kids.

Equipped with his new tools, Trey set out to find places where he would be excited to work. He made a list of about fifty places that appealed to him.

Then I asked to him pick the top fifteen and do a deeper dive to gather even more information.

The second time through he asked:

- What is it they really do?
- What is their organization or corporate mission?
- What do they make, create or provide?
- Who works there, and what seems to be the culture?
- How do they talk about themselves in press releases, and how are they covered by the press?
- Are they financially sound? Do they have good funding sources?
- Where are they located?
- Are there any people I'd like to meet? What are their names?
- How can I contribute? How can I envision fitting in? What will I learn?
- Are there any people highlighted that might make a good contact in the future?

I had him keep track of all of this in his Google spreadsheet and by the end of the exercise a couple of weeks later, he had better defined his wants, had some organizations he was really excited about, and the names of some people he'd like to meet.

Trey's situation is not unique. Like many young people coming out of college, he was nervous, ambitious, and not sure about what he wanted to be or do.

But in doing this exercise, he realized that the prospect of getting work was not the big black hole he had imagined. By Reverse Engineering the Job Market he felt in control of what he wanted to go after and an idea of how to get there.

Interestingly, Trey landed the very first job he applied to.

How? By knowing himself, finding a company that fit his PCB and meeting people who could help turn his interest into an opportunity, Trey set himself up for success.

This can work for you, too.

Perhaps you aren't interested in working in the social sector as Trey was. But sites like Craigslist.org, Monster.com, CareerBuilder.com and many others are also great resources for finding interesting places to work. And they're also excellent jumping off points for finding other resources where you can discover more interesting companies.

> You'll find a list of great company, organization and job listings sites on my website www.carryapaintbrush.com

Remember, just because a company doesn't have any jobs posted on their website, it doesn't mean they aren't hiring. There can be a million reasons for this, but at the end of the day, if you find a company that you want to work for, you've won three-fourths of the battle.

Okay, Trey was fresh out of college, and at the possibilities for him were numerous. But what about someone who's been working for several years? Someone who is pretty ingrained in the kind of work that they do? Someone who has developed a specialty or an expertise, and maybe is hesitant to move away from that? Do they have the same potential as Trey? Well....of course they do!

Meet George. George lost his job in the latest round of layoffs at his financial services company. As the married father of three kids, George was feeling intense pressure to find a new job quickly. But as a financial professional out of work in during a market downturn, the pickings in the financial services industry were slim to nonexistent.

When I met him, George was despondent about his job prospects and highly stressed about how he would be able to support his family.

George had made the same mistake that many job seekers make. Since he had been working at a financial services company, he felt like he was only qualified to work at a comparable financial services company. Until he started working with me, he had never really considered anything else.

As we worked together, it turned out that George had Passions and Interests that spread way beyond just the financial service world. PCB in hand, George worked to Reverse Engineer the Job Market. He discovered an incredibly diverse list of companies where he would like to work: a public relations company, a biotech firm, a healthcare company, and even an alternative energy startup.

Each one of those companies, though seemingly divergent, had one thing in common. They all needed someone in the organization to strategize, manage, and administer the financial matters of the company. From budget projections, to cash flow management and 401k investing, there are literally dozens of jobs within companies that require financially-oriented skills. George had just never thought this way.

After finding companies he was interested in, George made his short list and went back through to do a deeper dive. During his research he looked at company *About Us* pages and discovered he already had an acquaintance inside his favorite prospect company. By Reverse Engineering the Job Market, he found not only places he wanted to work, but people he knew who already worked there.

Reverse Engineering the Job Market can be fun and easy if you remember these simple strategies:

1) **Stay organized**. Whether you choose to use paper, an Excel spreadsheet, a Google online spreadsheet, or index cards stuck onto a wall, it's important to stay organized as you research companies and potential contacts.

2) **Set up a system that you will use**. There is no point in setting up a system and not using it. Your system should be flexible enough to allow for you to take notes, add new things to the lists, and track details (see the exercises at the end of this chapter for how to do this).

3) **Explore**. The point of Reverse Engineering the Job Market is to allow you to explore various areas of the working world. If you start off on Monster.com, and find yourself on a listing that was submitted by a job placement firm,

open another browser tab or window so that you can explore what other companies that placement firm represents.

You never know which path will lead you to something new and interesting. Keep track of places you want to go back to revisit in your tracking system. Sometimes you may end up in a rat-hole, but you probably discovered some interesting things both about yourself and the job opportunities while you were doing it. Make sure this doesn't happen too often.

4) **Work smarter, not longer**. As you spend time Reverse Engineering the Job Market, you will begin to recognize the difference between fruitful and unfruitful paths. Recognizing an unfruitful path early gives you a real advantage in searching for interesting companies. You'll spend more time investigating companies that are good potential matches for you rather than companies that hold no future possibility.

5) **Be disciplined**. Whether you dedicate three hours a day, three days a week for a period of three weeks or any other combination of time and frequency, the trick is to be disciplined about committing time to this process. Like trying to improve your cardiovascular strength requires frequent and consistent physical training, discovering your career path takes real committed time. Start by giving up something that requires a set amount of time and take that time to do this work. Know that whatever time sacrifice you make is an investment in your future. Your happy future. Work hard and you *will* see results.

Once you have Reverse Engineered the Job Market and know the companies that you're interested in pursuing, it's time to start meeting the people who can help you get "In." Do the exercises on the next page so that we can get started.

Chapter 10 Exercises

Reverse Engineer the Job Market

Reverse Engineering means you're going to take something apart and put it back together in a different way. And there's really no trick to learning how to do it. You just need to start. Here are some ideas to help you get going:

1) Assign yourself a four-hour chunk of time. This is important because I want you to feel like you have the freedom to do this badly at first, and then get better at it as you spend more time doing it.

2) Follow the steps outlined in this chapter to set up systems to keep track of everything including:

   First pass research
   - Name of company.
   - What they do.
   - Why I'm excited about them.
   - What I can imagine doing if I worked there.
   - The URL.
   - How I found them.

   Deep Dive Research
   - What is it they really do?
   - What is their organization or corporate mission?
   - What do they make, create or provide?
   - Who works there, and what seems to be the corporate culture?
   - How do they talk about themselves in press releases, and how are they covered by the press?

- Are they financially sound? Do they have good funding sources?
- Where are they located?
- Are there any people I'd like to meet? What are their names?
- How can I contribute? How can I envision fitting in? What will I learn?
- Are there any people highlighted that might make a good contact in the future?

3) Pick a job posting site (Monster.com, Careerbuilder.com, VolunteerMatch.com or any other site you can identify), and find where company profiles are listed.

4) In the search field, put the name of the city or cities where you are looking to work, or if you don't know where you want to work, use the *browse all companies* function.

5) Explore!

Chapter 11

Find an "In" Person

So you know who you are, what you want to do, and some companies and organizations where you'd like to do it. Now what?

It is time to start meeting and building relationships with the people who can help make your career goals into a reality.

What an "In" Person Can Do For You

One of the basic tenets of this book is that building a career isn't about applying for jobs and hoping you get them. It's about figuring out *what* you want to do, and then researching *who* is already doing it. Finding "In" people to help you get to the next stage of your career development is one of the cornerstones of Career Artistry.

Imagine if, in my John Schlesinger story, that I had sought out banking executives in hopes of getting work in the film business. Makes no sense! An "In" person is someone who is already *in* the business or *in* the field who can help open the door for you.

I want you to consider this: whether you seek that person out, or happen to meet them at a party, conference or event, being *open* to new people, new directions and new ideas is an essential piece of learning how to make this methodology work for you.

As the Artistic Director of Your Own Career, you never know who you might meet, and how much impact a single "In" person encounter can have on getting what you want.

The Power of a Single Person To Change Your Life

I met Steve in 1993 when I went to visit family in Boston over the holidays. During a casual party conversation, Steve asked me if I could work on any project in the world, what it would be. It was a great question. I hadn't really thought about it before.

At the time, I was writing and producing movies in Hollywood. But as a full-time Career Artist, there were always things in the back of my mind that I had imagined might be fun to work on. Here's what I told him.

"I've always wanted to create a spherical pod that you sit inside on a stationary bicycle. As you pedal, you're *inside* a 360-degree movie and you're riding through the streets of Paris! When you turn the handlebars to the right, you turn right in the movie. When you pass a bakery, it smells like bread," I said, enthusiastically adding, "Now you probably think I'm crazy."

As it turned out in the world of Creating Opportunities for Luck to Happen, **that one statement changed the direction of my career life forever**.

Steve happened to know some people at Stanford University who were creating "interactive movies that you experience while riding cardiovascular gym equipment." I couldn't believe it. I thought my idea was pretty off the wall, but it turns out that Steve knew some folks who wanted to bring movies and technology together. The techie in me was thrilled, and Steve offered an introduction.

The guys at Stanford were hosting a brainstorming session the following week in Palo Alto, California, and after an initial phone call, I was invited to attend.

That session turned into a writing assignment for me, as I was asked to write the company's very first interactive movie. It was through the process of writing the script that I discovered the nascent world of interactive (or as it was called then, *New*) media. None of this would have been possible if I had not been *open* to an intriguing question from a stranger at a party.

During the following February, I attended the Sundance Film Festival in Park City, Utah where I met Alex. Sharing a chairlift up the slopes one afternoon, Alex asked me what I was working on, and I explained the Stanford project. Alex, completely coincidentally, worked at one of the first interactive media firms in Los Angeles as a producer. She was working on a huge project interactive TV project for Time-Warner Cable. And…they needed a technical writer to create the tutorials for using the system. Was I interested?

I had no idea what I was getting myself into, but I agreed to meet Alex's team. I explained to them that I wrote screenplays and *had little* experience in technical writing and New Media. They replied that *no one had a lot* of experience in New Media. I was hired.

Unexpectedly, my docket was full of interactive media projects. And although it felt strange to have my feet slipping out of the film business into this new interactive world, it was fascinating and exciting. As a Career Artist, I have lived my life flowing where the Paint on the canvas has told me to go. I decided to take a leap and see where it led.

The Time-Warner project was being built by Silicon Graphics, a well-known technology innovator in San Jose, California. My job was to write a tutorial so that users could get help using the new system.

My contract was structured such that I only got paid per tutorial section. The problem was that no one was assigned to design how the system worked, so there was nothing for me to write about.

You can imagine my dilemma. I was scraping the proverbial bottom of the barrel and needed to find a way to get paid.

Armed with my engineering background, a basic interface concept call a "carousel," and a burning need, I put pen to paper and started mapping out how the system would work. From there I could write the accompanying tutorial, and get paid.

At first, the LA company was furious with me. How dare I "design" the interface for the system? That was the boss's job. I explained that because the boss was out of town at the World Cup Soccer Tournament, that the design wasn't getting done, and I needed to get paid. Necessity had just added a new Skill to my toolkit.

Within a week's time, I was living out of a hotel room in San Jose and working onsite at Silicon Graphics.

John was the technical lead on the project at Silicon Graphics, and I soon found myself to be his equivalent on the design side.

It was John who introduced me to this new thing called the World Wide Web when Mozilla, the first graphics-based web browser, came out in 1994. John went on to become a successful Internet entrepreneur and I, completely captivated by this burgeoning field, pulled up my roots in LA and moved to the heart of the Dotcom movement in San Francisco.

None of this curving path from Hollywood to Silicon Valley would have been possible without some well-placed and well-intentioned "In" people along the way.

I want you to start meeting some "In" people. These are the people who know the industry you are trying to crack, the company you want to get into, or the person you want to meet. They might even open a door you didn't know existed. They are the oxygen of your working life.

Learning how to meet, connect with and cultivate these relationships is an essential part of creating the career you've always wanted.

Anyone Could Be a Valuable Connection

My point in all of this is that "In" people can affect your life in many, many ways, and it isn't hard to do. Finding an "In" person might be as simple as being open and talking to people when you're in public. To some of you, this might sound scary, but when you're friendly to a stranger, at a party, in a park, on a plane, most likely, they'll return your friendly conversation.

Here's a good example. In his book, *The Luck Factor*, Richard Wiseman tells the story of Barnett Helzberg, Jr., who, by 1994, had built a chain of highly successful American jewelry stores, with annual revenues of about $300 million. One day he was walking down the streets of New York when he heard someone call out to a "Mr. Buffett." Helzberg thought that the person might be referring to Warren Buffett, the famous American investor. Helzberg decided to take a gamble and introduced himself to the stranger who had been called "Mr. Buffett" and discovered the man actually *was* Warren Buffett. A year later, all because of a chance meeting on the streets of New York City, Helzberg sold his company to Buffett.

The important lesson here is that people, those you know, and those you have yet to meet, are key to helping you create the future you want. Like so much of my story, I never imagined that a conversation on a ski lift would lead me from the film industry to the Dotcom world. You just never know.

So when you go to events, hang out with friends, or talk with family and colleagues, keep in mind what it is you want to be creating for yourself. Then, when someone asks, "What is your dream project?" or "What do you want to do next," you have an idea to share, a conversation to start, or the name of a person you are dying to meet. By sharing this information, you're giving people an opportunity to help you, which, as you'll learn in the next chapter, is a really important thing.

If you've been smart and worked hard at Reverse Engineering the Job Market, you now have a list of organizations and people that you would like to have a direct connection to. You've gone through the staff, management, and board of director's lists to see if you know anyone, or know anyone who might know someone. Feel free to share your list with family, friends, teachers, advisors, and your Mentor. Ask anyone who you think might have a connection, even if it's very loose, to the person or organization you want to meet.

If you can't find a direct connection, try using LinkedIn. LinkedIn (www.linkedin.com) is a professional networking site where millions of people are connected through a variety of shared work experiences, education, and people in common. It's an amazing way to gain access to people with whom you aren't directly connected.

Take Tammy, for example. Tammy was interested in meeting someone from Chronicle Books, a group she had targeted as a potential publisher for a project she was working on. Using LinkedIn, she searched for people who had included Chronicle Books in their list of past or current employers.

The search results showed Tammy that she was only "one step" away from the person in charge of Chronicle's acquisitions department, connected through a good friend from a previous job.

So she wrote to her friend and asked that an introduction be made. Within twenty-four hours, Tammy was on the phone with the person she wanted to meet at Chronicle.

This story is a typical and quite repeatable way of getting introduced to the people you want to meet. Your job is to make sure you have a LinkedIn profile that 1) details what you're interested in doing and 2) is "linked" to as many connections as possible. This way, when you're looking to make contact with someone new, you can use your LinkedIn network.

Facebook works in a similar way. People use Facebook "status" posts to ask for contacts and introductions all the time, and a new app called BranchOut is becoming a version of LinkedIn on Facebook.

Building your "In" people list is a lifelong activity, so I encourage you to always be prepared. Always have your business card handy. Offer to exchange contact information with people you find interesting, and stay in touch. Remember, those aren't just business cards. They're opportunities. And you never know when you might run into someone who can serve as a new hub in your network.

Chapter 12

Network by 5s

Creating Opportunities for Luck to Happen is a lot like the fairy tale of the princess who had to kiss a lot of frogs to find her prince—you need to paint a lot of doors to make lucky things happen.

I didn't know this when I arrived in Los Angeles in early January of 1989. After two years in London, it was time to come home and make a go of working in the U.S. I parked all of my belongings at my folk's house in Boston and bought a six-week round-trip ticket to LA. Basically, I was giving myself six weeks to break into the hardest business in the world. I was an idiot. I knew no better, and that's probably the reason I was successful.

In LA, I crashed on a friend's couch and made an appointment to see the one person whom I knew in the city—a theater producer from New York named Barbara Ligeti.

Barbara was in LA producing David Rabe's play, *Hurly Burly*. I went to her office one evening to say "hi," and catch up. While I was waiting in her lobby, a man came in and sat down next to me. Larry and I got talking. He, too, was waiting for Barbara.

He asked me my story, and I told him I was new in town, that I was just back from London where I had worked for John Schlesinger, and that I was looking to get into the film business in LA.

I *didn't* tell him that I had a round-trip ticket. He asked for my résumé and I gave him one. That was on a Thursday around 5:00 p.m.

When the phone rang in my friend's apartment early Monday morning, I could barely open my eyes. I had been smacked down with an awful flu and had been bedridden the whole weekend.

When the woman on the other end of the phone identified herself as Bettina Viviano, Director of Development for Steven Spielberg's production company, Amblin Entertainment, I almost fell out of bed.

Unbeknownst to me, Larry had been my "In" person. At a Super Bowl party the previous day, Larry had run into Bettina and she happened to mention she was looking for a new assistant in Spielberg's development office. Larry told her about me and faxed my résumé to her Monday morning.

Suddenly I was on the other end of the phone with someone in the inner circle of Hollywood. And though I didn't really know what development meant, when she asked if I could come in to meet, I jumped at the chance to say "Yes."

I drove onto the Universal Studios lot (I still have my drive-on pass that says Susanne Goldstein to see Steven Spielberg) to meet Ms. Viviano. She was a little bit older than me, with long blonde hair and a vivacious personality.

As I talked with her, I figured out that development people (mostly women called "D" girls) help shepherd scripts from draft to fully developed screenplays.

Specifically, it's a director of development's job to get the script in the right condition so that a studio will put up the financing to make it into a movie.

As her assistant, I would be responsible for vetting new scripts, writing "coverage," and determining their worthiness and financial viability. I had no idea how to do any of this. I didn't even know what "coverage" was. But that didn't stop me from telling her I could absolutely do it.

I know that this might seem like I was flying by the seat of my pants, and for the most part, that's true. But I knew I could figure out what "coverage" was and how to write it. I didn't want to get kicked out of the game so soon, so I had to find a way to stay in it.

So I said, "Yes." In a panic, and using my survival instincts, I asked her to share a copy of some already written "coverage" so that I could match how the document was formatted. It was a risk. But it paid off.

Bettina handed me the sample, a few scripts to cover, and sent me home to work. I studied the samples and quickly taught myself what I needed to do. By staying quick on my feet, using my smarts and taking a well-calculated risk, I was still in the running.

The next day I faxed my "coverage" to her and went back to the Universal lot. A night of reading scripts and writing coverage made me I realize that I didn't want to be a "D Girl." It was not for me. And though I would have been thrilled to work for Amblin, *I knew this job would not make me happy.* But how was I going to explain this to Bettina? And how could I convert this great bit of fortune into something bigger?

Political commentator and analyst Chris Matthews, has a chapter in his brilliant book, *Hardball: How Politics is Played Told by One Who Knows the Game* called, "It is Better to Receive Than to Give."

Matthews tells the story of Ross Perot's landmark 1992 bid for the U.S. Presidency. In his "masterful strategy," Perot told the American people that he would run for the presidency on one condition—that "regular people would buck the two-party establishment, cut through the red tape and get his name put on the ballot of the fifty states."

Perot's strategy, Matthew's points out, exploited "a staple of human nature discovered four centuries prior by Florentine statesman, Niccolo Machiavelli. The more you invest in someone, the more committed you become to him."

In other words, the best way to get someone to *support you* is to get them to do something *for you*. Or, as Ben Franklin once famously said, "If you want to make a friend, let someone do you a favor."

As I sat down for my second meeting with Bettina Viviano, I was certain that this job was not the right one for me, but I was not certain what to do next. After some discussion, Bettina and I came to the same conclusion. This wasn't a good match, and that we'd like to be friends.

We sat for a moment in silence when it occurred to me that having Bettina as my new friend was even better than having her as my boss. I decided to ask her a favor.

"You know," I said, "I'm new in town and don't know anyone. As a favor, would you be willing to introduce me to *5 of your colleagues who might be willing to talk to me for 5 minutes about what they do so that I can get a lay of the land?"*

She gave an immediate "Yes," and that day I walked off of the Universal Studios lot with a new friend and five new Hollywood people to contact.

By the end of the next week, while my car was whisking its way across the country, C.O.D. from Boston, I had already met for 5 minutes, with 5 people from Columbia Pictures, Disney Studios, and Warner Brothers.

Unbeknownst to me, I had pulled a "Ben Franklin."

And although I had only asked each person for 5 minutes of their time, each meeting went on for quite a while. Now I want you to note a couple of things: 1) When calling to make the appointment, I literally asked for a 5 minute meeting, 2) I asked them to tell me about themselves and did *not* tell them I was looking for a job, and 3) I just listened.

The funny thing is that by being a good listener and letting people talk about themselves, they end up thinking that you're wonderful. By showing genuine interest in them without asking for anything in return, you are giving them the affirmation that all humans need. And because of this, they will take an interest in you.

Eventually, each person I met asked about me. I shared that I was new in town and looking to land a job in the business. They asked for my résumé, which I happily gave them, and then I asked a favor. *Would they mind introducing me to 5 friends or colleagues who might be willing to meet with me for 5 minutes?* With each "Yes," my network grew.

This is how Networking by 5s was born. By the time I had been in Hollywood for five weeks, I had met 54 people.

Those fifty-four people became my Career Network and I knew that if I were going to break into the business, it would be because one of them had decided to help me out. I made time to nurture these relationships, one at a time, by handwriting thank you notes, follow-up letters, or sometimes calling with more questions about their job. My main goal was to keep in touch with them and to show that I was grateful.

Six weeks to the day that I had met Bettina, the *luck finally struck*. Despite lots of meetings, and two job offers in television which I turned down, I was starting to get dismayed at my prospects. Yes, I know, I was an impatient twenty-four-year-old fool, and I felt ready to give up. Luckily, I didn't have to.

The hardest thing about the Career Artist's journey is getting started. The second hardest thing is not giving up. I promise that if you stay hopeful, focused and determined, these techniques will work for you too.

Late in the day I checked my voicemail. There was a message from Disney Studios about a new movie they were staffing and needed to hire a director's assistant. The message went on to say that my résumé had been submitted for the job eleven times. Could I come in and meet the director?

Are you kidding me? Eleven of the fifty-four people I had met had heard about this job and recommended me. I was the "luckiest" girl in the world, though you know by now that there was actually very little luck involved here.

The next day I showed up on the Disney lot with my résumé, documents from working with John Schlesinger, and a pair of running shoes, just in case I got hired on the spot. I showed the director how I had made John's life easier during the *Madame Sousatska* shoot, and he hired me on the spot. I had broken into Hollywood.

Networking by 5s has proven, time and again, to be the most effective way I know to get connected with the people who can help you in your career. Whether you are trying to break into movies, software or hotel management, Networking by 5s works.

Like Reverse Engineering the Job Market, this is a *technique that you can adopt* to help you fast track your progress. In traditional job seeking, you are looking for jobs openings that exist and going after them. By Carrying a Paintbrush and Networking by 5s, you are looking to establish long-term relationships with the people who are doing the kinds of work you want to be doing, who know what job openings exist, what jobs are being created and, even better, have the ability to create a job for you if they think you're the right person.

Networking by 5s can be a blast. Even if you consider yourself shy, this simple technique can put you in front of people who can be of great help to you, in an environment where you can talk about things that you are passionate about. Here are some tips about Networking by 5s:

- **Networking is not a dirty word**. If I had a nickel for every person who thought networking was a bad thing, I would be a very rich woman. For some reason, networking has gotten a bad rap, and to some it means you are a "climber," a "brown-noser" or, "manipulative." This could not be farther from the truth.

- **Networking is no longer just for those with privilege and access.** In the past, knowing "In" people was confined to the privileged few who had enough influence to make connections. That's not true anymore. In today's world, offline and online connections can be made by anyone at anytime. Anybody can be connected. You need to embrace this reality to be successful at career development in the 21st century.

- **Networking is a vital and important part of life whether it's for social purposes or work purposes.** And in both cases, successful networks occur when the people at each node benefit from the relationship. Once you embrace the positive aspects of networking, you will learn that if you graciously and determinedly go after something that you are interested in, great things can happen.

- **Times have changed, so methods must change, too.** It might be harder to find and get a job now than in recent history, but it is wrong to think that opportunities don't exist. They do, and no matter how tough the market is, you can still get the kinds of jobs you want and will enjoy. By meeting the people who are engaged in the type of work you want to be doing, you will be top of mind when a new opportunity gets created.

In some cases, an opportunity might be created just for you. If you want to be the Artistic Director of Your Own Career, you need to take a bold and active approach. I've been know to suggest a role for myself at a company where

I think I can provide value. Know that passively waiting for someone else to get you a job is not going to get you anywhere. You have to help them help you.

- **Make the right "ask."** Successful people tend to be busy people. So the right kind of request for a meeting is crucial. See if you can get a direct phone number from your introducer. If you need to leave a voice mail, feel free to modify the following script:

"Hi, my name is [insert your first and last name here] and [insert the first and last name of your introducer here] suggested that I call you and that you might be willing to speak to me for five minutes about what you do. I'm interested in [insert the name of the field, industry, company here] and would be happy to come to your office to meet with you at your convenience."

Some of your scripts/emails/letters will be more successful at getting you on someone's calendar than others, so re-use the successful ones as you extend your network further and further. Notice when they aren't getting you where you want to go and think about what you can do to improve your chances for moving forward.

- **It's not all about you**. The basic tenet of Networking by 5s is simple: when you do get the opportunity to meet someone through the networking process, remember that it is *not* about you. To make Networking by 5s work, you need ignore your *need* for a job and focus on learning and gathering information from the person you are meeting.

By directing the conversation this way, you will have a chance to get to know people in the field, and give them a chance to get to know you. Most importantly, when they turn the conversation to you (which they will do if you are patient), you can show your enthusiasm and talk about your goals without either of you feeling like it was an "interview."

As I mentioned, the reason this technique works so well is that, in general, people love to talk about themselves. It's your job to have done some research about the person you are meeting, and be prepared to ask lots of good questions. (Google and LinkedIn are great resources for this type of research.) Sure, you can ask how they got where they are today, but wouldn't it be more powerful if you said, "I know that you used to work at [insert Company X here], how did you get from there to where you are now?"

Because I'm always fully prepared, engaged, and interested in the people I meet, almost all of my 5-minute meetings go close to an hour. By showing interest in them, they ended up interested in me. And when they're interested, you'll find that they remember you, invest in you, and try to help you. This is exactly what you want. So do your research, and remember it's not all about you.

- **It's all personal**. The Internet has helped each one of us create our own individualized world experience, yet, it has simultaneously made the world less personal. It has gotten to the point that, quite frankly, it's hard to differentiate one person from the next. One electronic résumé looks like every other electronic résumé and separating yourself from the pack becomes really difficult.

By finding a way to speak with people directly, you establish a personal relationship. Then when the time comes, your résumé or job application will stand out, not because you're more qualified than everyone else, but because the people reviewing these applications have a personal frame of reference for the kind of person that you are and the enthusiasm that you have.

It's not so unreasonable to think that, when they come across your résumé, they say, "Susanne Goldstein? Oh yeah, that new woman in town who had asked me for the names of five people in the business. I remember her; we had a really interesting conversation." Sometimes, that's all the incentive they need to pick your name out of the pile of a thousand others.

- **Stay open to everything.** When I met with Bettina Viviano, I had no idea what *development* or *coverage* were. But I went into the interview with an open mind, and I was willing to apply myself to learning something new for the sake of demonstrating my skill set. I'm not saying you should lie about the things you know, but sometimes the kinds of things people ask for are not as complicated as they seem.

You might not know the word coverage, but if she had said, "book report" or "summary," you would have. If you're open, you'll find a way to figure things out. The important thing is show no fear and be quick and creative on your feet.

Even if you have to practice your facial expressions in front of a mirror, I want you to present yourself in a way that says that you know what you're doing, and that when you don't, you can figure it out.

It not only shows people that you have confidence, but it's also a great opportunity for you to prove that you're creative enough to be qualified for the job, even if you don't really know how to do it yet.

- **Thank you notes say more than "thank you."** For every meeting you have, there *always* needs to be a next step. Whether it is a thank you, a follow-up on a topic that came up, the transmittal of your electronic résumé or a reminder of some action items that you discussed, a written greeting gives you an opportunity to show that you value the person's time and you know how to maintain professional relationships. I'm a fan of the written thank you note. It says a lot in an age where we seldom have stamps to send snail mail. But in our rapid speed digital age, email, depending on the situation, might be a better choice. In Chapter 26, I will tell you more about maintaining your Career Network and how it will become one of the most valuable assets in your working life.

- **Look and act the part.** When you arrive for a meeting, pretend you're already an employee. Dress appropriately, speak with confidence, carry your business card, and have clean copies of your résumé in a professional looking folder. Have a pen and paper upon which you can write down the names shared with you. I know most of this is pretty obvious, but you'd be amazed at how many people forget these simple things. And, whatever you do, don't forget your résumé! It's an essential part of your networking process. When asked for it, I would hand out three copies of my résumé and jokingly tell people to feel free to paper the walls with them. They always laughed but understood that I was asking them to spread it around.

- **Accept rejection with style.** Failure is awesome. It's one of the best teachers you can have. Whether you fail at getting someone to meet with you, have a bad meeting, or don't get a job that you were seriously being considered for, you need to celebrate your rejections almost as heartily as you celebrate your successes. So if you meet someone and they're not willing to share five (or any number) of names with you, have the guts to ask them for some constructive criticism so that you can learn what you could have done to win a referral from this person.

Of course, this Network by 5s technique isn't foolproof. In fact, no technique is. But it's a great way to create a baseline network from which you can get your foot in the door. And sometimes, that's all you really need to find the opportunity of a lifetime.

Chapter 12 Exercises

Find "In" People and Jump Start Your Career Network

If you're reading this book for the reason I think you're reading this book, *then* it is time for you to find your very first "In" person.

I know. It's terrifying. But as a friend once said to me before we jumped out of an airplane, "It's only scary if you look down."

So don't look down.

Take time to think about specific people who might be able to help you "break in" to your chosen industry. Create a list of those people and include their phone numbers and contact information. Next, you'll set up meetings with all the people on your list.

To jump-start your efforts, make sure to at least include:

- Someone you already know well who might be able to help you brainstorm people who you can put on your networking hit list.

- Someone you know "sort of" but not well. A little outside of your comfort zone, but still a connection through a connection.

- Some you don't know at all. Perhaps someone you found listed on a website for an organization that interests you, or someone you read about on the web.

From your "In" people, you'll start to Network by 5s and begin to build your Career Network.

But before you begin, here's another truth about life in the 21st century I want to share with you.

People don't use the phone enough.

Perhaps you think I'm nuts for saying that—everyone always seems to have a cell phone glued to their ears. But the truth is that when it comes to making contact with new people, people are afraid of the phone.

Don't be. The phone is a great way to reach out to someone new. You're probably most inclined to send an email, but email could get marked as spam, go unnoticed, or get deleted. Plus, you don't know if someone received your message.

A phone call or voice message that includes the name of your introducer not only gives credence to your call, but associates your voice with your request. This form of human contact has better potential for a stranger to take an interest in you.

If you get someone on the phone, make the simple ask for five minutes of their time. If you get their voice mail, leave a short prepared message and tell them you will follow up later that day (which of course, you will do).

If the concept of cold-calling a stranger absolutely terrifies you, consider asking your "In" person for an email introduction (like the one I wrote for Dave in Chapter 6). This helps because it allows you to immediately follow up from the introduction (remember this is *your* responsibility), thank your introducer, and make a good first impression.

Whatever method you choose to use, now is the time to get started.

Here's what I want you to do:

1) Make a pledge to yourself to reach out to 3-5 new people every week (more if you are ambitious!).

2) Research each person, devise a strategy, and develop an introductory story for each contact.

3) STOP thinking about each new contact as the scariest thing in your life.

4) Pick up the phone and make the call, or type the email and press "Send." Just make it happen.

Remember, by Claiming Your Career As Your Own, you signed up for being in control of your own destiny. Stepping outside of your comfort zone might be difficult and challenging at first. But it's something you can overcome. Start now!

Chapter 13

Do the Unexpected

Even for some of the best networkers on the planet, there are occasions where you just don't know anyone who can make an inroad to the person you're trying to meet. For most people this would seem a daunting issue, but not to Matt.

I met Matt when I was working as an assistant at Disney Studios in Hollywood. Hollywood assistants are young, ambitious grunts who are would-be movie producers, studio executives, directors and more. Matt and I met through fellow grunt, Lee Rosenthal, who chronicled some of our exploits in an article in *Details Magazine*. Lee, now Executive VP of Physical Production at Paramount Pictures, Matt and I were part of the gang of Hollywood up and comers who attended a "university" we fondly called Disney U., and cut our teeth in film production.

It was impossibly hard, totally cut-throat, and incredibly fun. Having a thick skin was necessary as you assisted a Hollywood bigwig by day, and surreptitiously scrambled to get your own projects off the ground by night.

Matt was the child of a studio executive with a lot to prove. Determined not to "make it" on his dad's coattails, he was uber focused and tenacious about making his mark. But Hollywood is full of Matts. And the question becomes, *how can you stand out in a world where everyone is trying to stand out?*

Although it may seem that trying to get a project going in Hollywood is completely different than trying to get a job, nothing could be further from the truth.

In fact, Hollywood just might provide the best model possible for explaining how to Create Opportunities and advance your career.

In Hollywood, there are no job postings. And as you learned in the previous chapter, everything happens based on *who you know, who knows you, who the people you know know*, and how much you can get them to notice you and invest in you. To get a job in Hollywood, there are no website listings, no applications to submit, and no formal interview process. This might explain why it's so difficult to break in. Traditional methods don't work.

Matt was the master of untraditional methods. He had the rights to a screenplay called *Surfwise* about the iconoclastic Paskowitz family and their search for the perfect wave. Determined to get the movie made, Matt set his mind on connecting with every producer in town who had an interest in surfing. Specifically, he wanted to get the script in front of Brian Grazer, an avid surfer who would later go on to produce *Apollo 13* and the TV show *24*.

Getting in front of Brian was no easy feat, and Matt decided to go all out in his effort to get noticed. He purchased a used surfboard, had it custom painted with a quote from Paskowitz patriarch, "Doc," and attached the completed screenplay to the surfboard. He called a messenger service and had the surfboard delivered. Though Grazer passed on the movie (Mark Cuban's company, Magnolia Entertainment eventually produced it in

2007, fifteen years later) Matt's is a great story about Doing the Unexpected.

Many of you might feel that you could never pull off this type of entrepreneurial, non-conformist behavior. Or perhaps you don't have the money to purchase surfboards for strangers. Know that Doing the Unexpected doesn't have to create such a spectacle.

Verna is a nationally recognized expert and speaker on diversity issues and recruiting in the workplace. But that's not how she started her career.

After running the Black Student Organization at her university, Verna went on to study and then practice law, signing on with one of the big corporate firms in Boston. But something didn't feel right. Practicing law, it seemed, wasn't what made her happy. She craved to speak to, and motivate crowds. She wanted to feel like she was impacting peoples' lives. After six years of practicing law, she quit.

Not knowing what was next, Verna contemplated many options, including journalism. At the time, Liz Walker was a successful, well-known television news anchor, and like Verna, a woman of color. Verna admired Liz and thought she'd be a great role model. Verna wanted to talk to her, but because of who Liz was, she assumed she'd never have the chance to meet her, and if she did, Liz would never talk to her.

Verna proved her negative self-speak wrong when one day while walking in downtown Boston, she spotted Liz waiting for a cab. Without thinking twice, Verna walked up to her and said, "There you are!"

"Excuse me?" Liz replied.

"I've really wanted to talk to you for a long, long time!"

"Oh, really?" Liz said hesitantly.

Verna knew that this was her moment. So she seized it. She explained that she was a lawyer, that she had hated it, and that she had just quit her job and was looking for a new career.

She told Liz, "You're such an inspiration—I watch you on the news every night. You're the perfect person for me to talk to about working in TV news."

Liz smiled and replied, "So it's your fault that I've been standing here so long waiting for a cab!"

Not only did Liz agree to meet with Verna after their chance encounter, but to this day, they remain colleagues and close friends.

Yes, walking up to a stranger can be terrifying. But instead of asking yourself, "What's the worst thing that could happen?" ask yourself, "What the best thing that could happen?" You just never know and you won't find out unless you step outside of your comfort zone and try.

I encourage you to think differently about how you can manifest things for yourself in the world. You see, **at the end of the day, no one is looking out for your career but you.** Therefore you're the one who has to put yourself out there, take the risks, and reap the rewards.

You don't have to be as dramatic as Matt was, or as courageous as Verna was, or even as daring as I was in sitting for two weeks in the lobby of the National Theatre. But you can stretch your own boundaries and ask yourself to be more creative about how you go about pursuing your work life. By being bold and seeking out opportunities where no one else is looking, you can expand your network, expand your horizons, and create more and more Opportunities for Luck to Happen.

Chapter 14

Getting a Job is a Full-time Job

In the opening line of his classic self-help book, *The Road Less Travelled*, M. Scott Peck M.D., tells us that, "Life is difficult." He goes on to say that once you understand this truth, you realize that life being difficult shouldn't get in your way.

The same is true for creating the career you've always wanted. Or in simpler terms, finding the job you always wanted. Finding a job is hard. Period. But you don't have to make it feel hard. Instead of thinking of job searching as an onerous undertaking, think of it as a fun challenge.

Imagine for a moment that your full-time job is to *meet and talk to interesting people*. To be 100 percent successful at this job, all you have to do is have great conversations and learn cool things.

Now apply this same thinking to your career development. If you change your perspective, and view developing your career as an opportunity to meet cool and interesting people rather than hard work, it won't feel like an overwhelming and impossible task to master. In fact, you might enjoy it as much as I do.

There are, however, several important things to keep in mind as you go through this process. Recently, while doing a career development workshop at a local university, a student raised his hand and told me a story. The previous night he had spent an *"entire hour writing personalized cover letters and applying to twenty jobs on Monster.com."* At the end of the process, he told me he was completely exhausted, and now two days later, he was despondent that he hadn't heard back from anyone.

I couldn't help but laugh. Here are a few things I told him:

1) **Getting a job is a full-time job.** It really is. And if you think it's any easier than that, you're in for a big surprise. If you're currently in a job and looking for a new job, your nights and weekends are going to be taken over by your quest. If you don't have a job currently, your new job is to find a job, and you should spend a typical workday (eight to ten hours) researching companies, meeting new folks, following up on meetings, and connecting with new leads.

   My student in the above scenario thought that his one-hour investment was enough to find a job. That's why I laughed. If you really want a new gig, you have to really work for it and put enough skin in the game to make it happen.

2) **Work harder than everyone else.** Take my student above as a great example. If he is typical and thinks that he can get a job by spending an hour submitting résumés, then it won't be hard for you to work harder than he does.

   I consider it a decent amount of time to spend twenty minutes researching a company for the first time. I will also spend twenty minutes researching a person I am going to meet. And when it comes to writing introductory emails, follow-up letters, and thank you notes, I will spend up to thirty minutes per, making sure that I have read and re-read what I've written to make certain that I'm saying exactly what I want to say (remind yourself about Communicating Like a Pro in Chapter 6).

3) **Stay organized.** When you learned about Reverse Engineering the Job Market, you hopefully set up a system for yourself to keep track of the companies you're interested in. In a similar way, it's important to stay organized about your correspondence back and forth with people. Using the folder system of your email program is a great way to do this. I suggest creating a folder called "Career Development" and within it, create a folder for each company (or person) you're corresponding with. Keep copies of your sent items in each appropriate folder so that you can view the entire thread of a conversation, and be able to track who wrote to whom last.

Another trick is to use a calendar. It's a great way to track your appointments and add reminders to follow up with someone at a certain date or time. For instance, if you get an email that says, "Call me next week," you can put a reminder in your calendar. Or, and this happens a lot, someone says, "I'll get back to you by Friday." Put a note in your calendar for Monday reminding yourself that they were supposed to check in. If you still haven't heard by Wednesday, feel free to forward (not reply) their email back to them and say "Per our correspondence below, I'm checking in to see if you've had any time to look into this matter further?"

What you don't want to have happen is that you miss out on a great opportunity because someone somewhere dropped the ball. By staying organized, you can make sure this doesn't happen.

4) **Learn from mistakes.** No doubt somewhere along the way in the Career Development process, you're going to say

something stupid, forget a meeting, not recognize the face of a person you've already met, send a typo-filled email or do something else that appears untoward. The best way through these situations is to apologize, learn from your mistake, and move on. Try not to fixate on it. In truth, it's doubtful that anyone else thought it as egregious as you do. So forgive yourself, move on, and don't do it again.

5) **View rejection as an opportunity to grow.** I know you hate hearing it, but failure *is* awesome. If you don't get a job you were seriously interviewing for, see if you can speak to the hiring manager to understand what you could have done differently to secure the position.

If they're willing, ask them what qualities the selected candidate possessed to make him or her the winning choice. Accept failure as an opportunity to learn. Be gracious and grateful. Remember, all of these people are part of your Career Network and you never know when you might run into them again in the future.

Sometimes rejection comes in the form of silence. *Not* hearing from a person or a company where you submitted your résumé is as disheartening as being outright rejected.

But keep this in mind: Every person you're trying to reach is busy. Following up on an unanswered email is very appropriate, as long as it doesn't turn creepy. And after one or two inquiries (over the period of a couple of weeks) go unanswered, it's time to graciously move on. Perhaps the hiring manager was deluged with prospect résumés and didn't have time to get back to you, or the executive was traveling on business and couldn't respond.

Despite feeling like you're flapping aimlessly in the wind, you have to get comfortable with the discomfort of not knowing. It's okay. You will survive. Just keep in mind that *when someone doesn't hire you it's not personal.* They're making a business decision, and you need to learn to separate your personal feelings from your professional feelings so that it doesn't sting so badly.

Consider the contestants on American Idol—each year over 100,000 hopefuls audition to be the next big thing in music. And each year, only one person wins. Does that mean that the person who got fourth place should feel untalented and bound to fail? Absolutely not! They are better than 99,996 who auditioned, and that's a huge success. Just because you didn't land the job you wanted, doesn't mean you're untalented, unlikeable, and will never land the job you want. Remember, it's not personal, it's business.

6) **Stop complaining.** No one likes a complainer. If you're complaining about *getting* a job, how are you going to be when you *have* a job? No one wants to hire a complainer. Plus, what is it you're actually complaining about?

Do yourself a favor, regardless of your age, don't be one of those people who feels that they deserve for things to be easy and always go their way. It's a great disservice to yourself and it's not going to endear you to anyone at all. The best thing you can do for your career development is enjoy the process, engage positively, and get things done!

Now look, I'll admit that some of these points seem a little harsh, and you can bet that this student wasn't exactly thrilled to hear them. But the fact is that in the working world, no matter your level of experience, you have to be mature—not just in age, but in demeanor, as well. Remember, these companies aren't hiring your skills; they're hiring *you*. The person. They need to be able to work with *you* and count on *you*. So be professional. It's that simple. If you can do that, you'll be well on your way.

Chapter 15

Where You're At and Where We're Headed

In the first three parts of this book, you've learned a lot about yourself. You've learned that a career is something you can create and be in control of. You've identified who you are in the working world, and you've had an opportunity to develop a framework for the type of work you would be happy doing.

You've also learned how to Create Opportunities for yourself—how to encourage Luck to Happen. You are building your Career Network, meeting people who are investing in your future, and doors are opening.

The next phase of your journey is about where you're headed, and how you can best prepare yourself for that fortunate day when you're asked to interview for your dream job.

Part 4 is dedicated to helping you prepare yourself to step into the new world that your future promises and convert a lucky moment into a real, paying job.

Part 4

Paint Yourself into the Picture: Be Prepared When Luck Strikes

"Luck is a matter of preparation meeting opportunity."

- Oprah Winfrey

Chapter 16

What to Do When Luck Strikes

You've been creating Opportunities for Luck to Happen every time you reach out to someone new, get an introduction from a person in your Career Network, or have a chance meeting with someone who takes an interest in your future. What makes an Opportunity for Luck turn into true luck is a question of timing, conviction and perseverance.

You can never know when luck is actually going to strike, and even the most committed Career Artists get down, frustrated and start to lose faith.

I've had my down moments too. Back in Los Angeles, that day I got that call about the Disney interview, I was actually consoling myself at the mall doing a little "retail therapy." I was seriously considering buying a pair of boots I couldn't afford (in order to distract myself from my worries) when I checked my voice mail and heard the good news.

We all get frustrated. But eventually luck does strike, and when it does, you need to be ready.

Being Prepared When Luck Strikes means you know exactly what to do, what to say, and how to act when you get called in to interview for your dream job.

Don't panic.

Just like in the previous sections of the book where I explained in detail how to discover who you are, what you want to be in the world, and how to meet the people who can help you get there, in this section of the book I'm going to make sure that you know exactly what is required to convert your lucky moment into a real, paying job.

Prepare 10 Times Smarter

To do this well, to be able to demonstrate how you're the perfect new hire, you need to be *prepared*.

And when I say prepared, I'm talking about fully-engaged, full-throttle, exhaustive preparation. This takes effort and time, and will hands-down be one of the key differentiators between you and other candidates who are applying for the job.

For the record, if you think that you can waltz into a job opportunity unprepared, you're in for a harsh and unhappy outcome. So let's avoid that.

What I want you to do is prepare ten times smarter than anyone else. And by smarter I don't mean IQ smart. I mean prepared smart. Hardworking smart. Informed smart. Anticipatory smart. Here's what I mean:

- For every minute that someone else has spent getting to know the company, I want you to have spent ten.
- You have a clear understanding of the company's mission, strategy, structure, challenges, and outlook.
- Some of your industry contacts have offered their perspective about the organization.
- You've reflected on some challenges the organization may face, and have brainstormed solutions.

By preparing rigorously, I guarantee you that you will:

- Walk into the room with calm confidence and charisma.

- Understand who you are and demonstrate what you can bring to the table.

- Control your nerves and act like this is just another one of your Networking by 5s meetings.

- Get your interviewer to like you.

In the next chapters, I'm going to show you how to do all of this. So let's get started.

Chapter 17

Paint Memorable Stories

There is nothing more important during the interview process than knowing how to talk about yourself and tell your stories. Storytelling draws people in, allows them to know you, and allows you to present yourself in a valuable and compelling way.

Take a moment and think about a dinner or an event you were at recently. Was there one person there that held everyone's attention because of their ability to tell intriguing, captivating stories? Whether the story was about a recent fishing trip, a fight with a co-worker, or a humorous experience at a restaurant, a great storyteller has the ability to transform the most mundane episode into an extraordinary tale.

Using Storytelling as an Interviewing Tool

It's no difference in interviewing. And with practice, you can learn how to become an adept teller of your own stories—from describing your greatest strength, to your desire to work in a particular field, to how you're addressing a weakness. As a technique, it can be used to answer just about any question an interviewer can throw at you.

Unfortunately, not everyone is a natural-born storyteller. Especially not Daryl.

Daryl is a smart, dedicated husband and father who had been laid off from his job working as a project manager for a networking company.

A former military officer, he had very limited experience with traditional interviewing since retiring. He had always found work through friends and referrals. Looking for work in a bad job market, a wife and two kids to support, Daryl was extremely anxious when he contacted me to help him prepare for an upcoming interview.

Our mock session was a challenge right from the start. It was clear as he answered each of my questions with a one-word, or one-sentence answer, that he didn't like talking about himself and didn't know how to tell his own stories.

What I realized is that Daryl needed a crash course in storytelling.

Every Story Has a Beginning, Middle, and End

As we learned in Chapter 6, using a 3-Act structure to write a great email is an extremely useful tool. I didn't make that up.

In fact, it was Aristotle, in his *Poetics*, who taught us about 3-Act structures and "plot."

Plot, he explained, is the most important part of a story. It is more important than the lead character, must not refer to things outside of the story that would confuse the listener, and must have a beginning, a middle, and an end.

To break this down into learnable storytelling skills, this is how I translate Aristotle's lesson to us.

First, when you tell a story, how you tell it should *focus on the progress of the plot* primarily, and your role in the story secondarily.

Second, as you tell the story, there must be a progression that takes the listener on a 3-Act journey from what I call Inception, through Action, to Resolution.

Act 1—Inception is where you introduce the plot of the story, what the situation is, and who or what is involved. Remember to include any pertinent background information so that your listener understands what is going on. This is your chance to "hook" your listener in. Make it interesting, impressive and bold.

In movie terms, this is when, in Star Wars, Luke Skywalker finds out his family has been killed and makes the decision to join the Rebel Alliance.

In your story, this is when, in answering the question, "tell me about how you dealt with a difficult situation at work" (for example), you would set up the situation, briefly explain the people or things involved, and describe the challenge you were facing.

Act 2—Action describes the steps you've taken to address the problem or issue described in the plot. This is where the story progresses, challenges or changes are recognized and decisions need to be made in order to influence, persuade or redirect outcomes.

In Star Wars, this is when Luke learns to fight with a light saber, frees Princess Leia, flees the Death Star and Obi Wan Kenobi dies.

In your story, this is when you would describe potential scenarios for resolving the difficult situation, what people or things you needed to consult with (or influence) in order to make a decision, and how you decided which way to go.

Act 3—Resolution is where the rubber hits the road. This is where your actions change the outcome of the plot. It is the progression of steps that you've taken to conclude the story and bring the listener to a place of closure.

In Star Wars, this is when Luke accepts his inner-Jedi, blows up the Death Star and saves the rebellion.

In your story, this is when you would describe how you implemented your solution, made sure that all issues surrounding the original challenge were resolved, and report any important outcomes.

In other words, you tell a 3-Act story that takes the listener on a journey, like in the diagram below.

Act 1 - Inception   Act 2 - Action   Act 3 - Resolution

Good storytelling draws us in, and we not only listen attentively, but we're eager to see how the story will resolve. As you become more aware of Aristotle's 3-Act story arcs, you'll start to understand why some people are such great storytellers.

Using Storytelling to Move Hearts and Minds

At the Democratic National Convention in 2004, a relatively unknown Illinois Senatorial candidate named Barack Obama told an amazing story, and inspired a nation. Whether you support Obama's politics or not, the fact is that his talent as a storyteller can move mountains.

From the humble beginnings of his grandparents to the unlikely marriage of his white, midwestern mother, to his Kenyan-born father, Obama helped us believe that anything was possible in America.

He was given an African name, Barack, or "blessed," because his parents believed that "in a tolerant America your name is no barrier to success." He quoted the Declaration of Independence and made us remember why our nation is so great, and how much work we have yet to do.

After capturing our hearts, he painted a picture of a future led by John Kerry, the Democratic Presidential candidate that year. But not many of us actually remember that part.

What Obama did that night was actually so much larger. He placed himself squarely in our collective conscious and became a significant player on the national political stage. His gift as a storyteller forever changed the color of American politics.

Great storytelling is a sure way of winning hearts and minds and, as demonstrated by President Obama, it's an incredible tool for advancing one's career.

So here are two things you need to know about using storytelling as an interviewing tool:

- Telling stories to friends and family and telling a story to an interviewer are very different. In telling stories to friends, the subject, or plot, of the story isn't particularly important.

In these situations, we tell stories to share our feelings, entertain, or relay something that happened. In an interview situation, the stories must be focused to answer a specific question, demonstrate a particular skill, or explain your background and experience.

- When telling a story with friends and family, the story can go on as long as you want, have many twists and turns, and not necessarily ever get to the end. In an interview situation, the stories must be relatively short (one to five minutes depending on the question or topic), address a specific issue, and have a point.

As you develop, write and practice your own stories at the end of this chapter, remember to keep these guidelines in mind and discover your own talent to move hearts and minds through story.

Using Storytelling to Show That You Can Think Critically

Okay, so it's probably the most overused word in all of interviewing. But being able to demonstrate that you can *think critically* is incredibly important during the interview process. It shows your interviewer that you can tackle complex issues with ease.

As you decide which stories to share during your interview, consider ones that demonstrate your ability to critically think about a challenge, and that you know how to:

- Observe and evaluate various parts of an issue.
- Prioritize their importance in regard to the problem you're trying to resolve.
- Draw conclusions based on your evaluation.

- Test your conclusions against relevant criteria and revise as necessary.

Meet Samantha. Samantha has a Ph.D. in Psychology and was interviewing for a job as a freshman social psychology professor when I met her. The school's program in Social Psych. had historically been weak, and Samantha was being brought in to see if she would be the right teacher to get the students more engaged and interested.

Through her research she discovered that the previous two professors gave uninspired lectures accompanied by dreary PowerPoint slides. For the students, the class had become about memorization, not learning.

During the interview, the dean asked Samantha how *she* would approach teaching the class. Samantha knew that this was a huge opportunity to make a great impression and show her ability to problem solve and think critically.

Here's the story she told him:

"In preparation for coming here today, I asked your assistant to share with me anonymous reviews of the past few semesters of teaching. In reviewing the survey results, I discovered that the students didn't feel engaged, were bored, and thought that the material was not relevant to them. I knew that in order to fix this, I would have to do something bold that would engage them in a fun way and reestablish the reputation of Social Psych as a course offering."

Samantha went on to give specific examples of the types of activities she wanted to bring into the classroom, and explained how she wanted to use magazines, TV, and YouTube to bring real cases to the students.

"After a few weeks, I plan on passing out surveys and conducting a focus group on how to improve the classroom experience for the students, and then adjust my approach accordingly."

The dean was duly impressed and within a few months of her hiring, hers was one of the most popular classes at the school.

Samantha's story provides a great lesson to anyone interviewing for a job. Instead of simply telling the dean what she wanted to do in the classroom, she demonstrated that she understood the challenges at hand, that she could devise a variety of solutions to solve the problem, choose a solution, put it into practice, and follow up with an evaluation of the effectiveness of the choices she made.

The important thing to remember is that demonstrating critical thinking is about revealing your thinking process, how you come to decisions, and how you evaluated their impact. Even if the story you tell isn't directly related to the job opportunity at hand, your interviewer will recognize and appreciate learning how your brain works.

The Story of You

The most important story of all is the story of *you*. Every person you meet is going to want to know who you are and what you've been up to. Lucky for you, you know. Once you figure out a compelling way to tell it, you will win over your interviewer.

Think about examples, episodes and experiences that paint a colorful picture of who you are. Think of the jobs you've had, the projects you've worked on, the community work that you've done. Ask yourself to imagine your life as a movie. What is the plot of the movie? Which parts would you highlight?

Your story should show your personality. Humor, self-reflection and enthusiasm are key. Use the 3-Act framework to give your narrative structure. And have fun. If you don't love the Story of You, who will?

As an example, here's the story I tell in answer to: "So tell me about yourself."

Act 1—Inception "I have a really crazy background. I have two degrees, one in mechanical engineering and the other in theater and film."

> *Note: People usually immediately stop me right here, to either say "Wow!" or some other comment showing that they are immediately intrigued. Try to think of a great starting line like this one.*

"When I first got out of school, I went to London where I worked at the National Theatre of Great Britain designing sets and a seating system for their experimental stage.

From there, I got into the film business. I started as an assistant and worked my way up to being a producer and screenwriter in Hollywood."

> *Note: People sometimes stop me here wanting to know if they've seen any of the movies I've made. Don't let*

an interruption throw you off track. Instead get energy from your interviewer's enthusiasm.

Act 2—Action "In the early 90s, before the Web, I was hired to write an interactive movie for a group at Stanford. They were making movies that people could *experience* while riding cardiovascular gym equipment.

It was at that time that I realized that in this new *interactive world*, writing and design were the same thing. I'd like to say I was really prescient back when I got my two degrees, but honestly, I was just lucky.

Act 3—Resolution "I got introduced to the Web in 1994, moved to San Francisco and became one of the early experience and user interface designers. Everyone wanted to get on the Web, and there weren't that many of us doing web stuff at the time. The venture capital guys were throwing money at anyone who had an idea, so I had all of these start-ups, working out of a garage, asking me to design a site for them. I'd ask them what they wanted the company to "*be when they grew up?*"

They didn't know how to answer, so I ended up developing a methodology for how to define, design and develop interactive products. And that's how I got to be doing what I'm doing today."

That's my story. It takes me two to four minutes to tell, and changes slightly depending on my audience. Sometimes, I'll tweak my which elements to include based on what I believe would be interest to my interviewer.

My story provides a lot of places for my interviewer to take the conversation, and is interesting enough to keep them enthusiastic and engaged.

This should be the same for you.

Even if your personal story isn't as varied as mine is, you can still find ways of making it interesting.

Perhaps your experience on the soccer field taught you to think differently about teamwork. Or you had a grandmother who brought you to volunteer at a food bank when you were a kid, and it inspired you to pursue a career in public service.

Remember that your palette as a Career Artist is full of color, and it is your job to paint stories and take your listener on a wonderful journey.

In the exercises that follow, take the time to develop your own stories. Great stories are critical to advancing your career, getting hired and stepping into a new job. Plus, they are yours to keep and use for the rest of your life.

I encourage you to write and then practice telling as many stories as you can imagine. With practice, you can become a master storyteller.

Chapter 17 Exercises

Prepare Your Stories

There are an infinite number of ways an interviewer can ask you a question, and there are lots of sites on the Internet to help you prepare. However, the best way to answer an interviewer's question is to tell a compelling story.

Use the following questions as a starting point:

- Tell me about you (The Story of You).

- What is your greatest strength?

- What do you consider a weakness? (don't say you work too hard—find a real weakness and mention what you are doing to address it).

- Tell me about your last job (this may include asking why you are leaving, or have left). If this is your first job, you may get asked about past volunteer or group activities.

- What can you do that other candidates can't? (this is your chance to show off your Special Sauce).

- Can you give me an example of when you had to think out of the box? (This is a great place to show off your ability to think creatively and critically).

- Tell me about a particularly challenging situation you have faced.

- Why are you interested in this position?

- What is your work style? (Tell them about how you work best when your primary assignments or tasks relate to your Contribution Style).

- Tell me about a moment of conflict and how you resolved it.

Think about your experiences and how they relate to the interview questions above. Use a 3-Act structure to draft your stories. Share them with a friend, a colleague, your mentor. Based on their feedback, revise and then finalize them.

Now it's time to practice. Practice your stories every day until they become natural to you. Practice them to yourself, in the mirror, to friends and family.

See if you can identify a trigger word to help you remember what story to tell to answer what type of question (this is why you should have plenty in your arsenal). For example, if you hear the word conflict or challenge, your "problem solving story" should just flow out of your mouth in a conversational and confident manner.

Remember that preparing your stories will benefit you in multiple ways.

- You'll feel more confident going into your interview.
- You'll have reminded yourself of all of the cool and interesting things you've done in your life
- You'll gain confidence in your ability to contribute.
- By practicing this structured form of storytelling, you'll become more adept at incorporating stories into all aspects of your life.

Chapter 18

Research an Organization in 60 Minutes or Less

I once heard a story about a person who walked in for a job interview, sat down and asked, "So, what exactly do you guys do?"

I was horrified, and honestly wondered if this was a story cooked up by human resource professionals to try to get candidates to better prepare.

Whether this particular tale is true or not doesn't matter. What does matter is that you can make no greater mistake than to walk into interview underprepared.

If you've been following my lead, you've done plenty of research *before* you even submitted your résumé. But now that you're being asked in the door, here's what you want to make sure you know.

> NOTE: For more in depth detail on how to research a company, visit my website www.carryapaintbrush.com

Understand Their Objective

An organization's objective amounts to what and who they are trying to be in the world—their raison d'être. In researching intention, you want to see if you can get a sense of not only what the company does, but in what way they do it.

For example, some energy companies are focused on traditional sources of power generation, and others are focused on "clean" energy production. Make sure you know their orientation and who they are. Here are several things you should consider researching:

- What are they trying to achieve?
- What is their mission statement?
- What are their main products or services?
- How do they make or get money?
- What's their culture?

Memorize the Basics

Knowing a company in as much detail as possible is never a bad thing. It helps prepare you for all sorts of questions and gives you a great foundation from which you can form questions to *ask your interviewer*.

For instance, if you find out that the company has three divisions, you can learn more about the division you might be working for. And if you don't know this information, it's a great question to ask.

Some company details are easier to get at than others, and privately held companies, in particular, are more difficult to research. Don't let that daunt you. There is enough information out there for you to cobble together a pretty comprehensive view. Here are a few things to think about:

- When were they founded?
- Are they establishment or cutting-edge oriented?

- Are they publicly or privately held? If public, check out stock price trends.
- How big are they, how are they structured, and where are they located?
- What is their financial status? Layoff history?
- Are there opportunities for advancement?
- Who are their big clients or customers?

Get Familiar with Who's Who

Getting to know the people who run and work at the company is enormously important, and in preparing for your first meeting, you'll want to know as much as you can about your interviewer. You'll also want to know about the people who are running and working at the company.

Once you get in the door, your gut will tell you whether it's a good fit or not. Before then, take time to learn about the people you'll be working for and with. The people you should investigate include:

- Your interviewer.
- The head of the company.
- Senior management.
- The board of directors or advisors.
- Potential teammates.

Define Their Customer

An organization delivers its products and services to others. It is crucial that you know going into your interview who those "others" are.

Here are five ways to discover an organization's audience (or target market, customer base, or user base to use a few other terms that describe the same thing).

- Look on the company's website and analyze the products and services they offer.
- Determine if they do business with consumers (known as business to consumer, or B2C). Or if they interact with other businesses (known as business to business, or B2B).
- If it is a non-profit, are they helping individuals (a mobile health clinic, B2C) or helping other organizations as they do good work in the world (supporting schools, B2B).
- Review their client or customer roster if available.
- Read customer testimonials and press releases.

By knowing this information, you are demonstrating your understanding of, and interest in, the company and are prepared to ask smart, compelling questions.

Investigate Their Competitors

Showing your interviewer that you are familiar with their competition will earn you good points. Since organizations often analyze their competitor's actions in comparison to their own, you can, through your research, determine who they consider to be in their headlights (a leader in the marketplace), or in their rearview mirror (a lagger in the marketplace).

Arming yourself with this information is great preparation. Both Yahoo! Finance and Google Finance offer "competitors" or "related companies" links for publicly traded companies. Privately-held organizations take a bit more work, but dig in hard and you'll find what you need.

Another reason to investigate competitors is much more selfish. If things don't work out with this company, but you're still interested in the field, the competitors might be a great place to try next. Familiarizing yourself with them now can only help you in the future.

Find Out Their Reputation

If a person works for Google, people will think they are super smart, cutting edge and have a cool, laid back California vibe. If a person works for GE, people will think that they have been through extensive training, understand great processes and like to work for a big corporate giant.

A company's brand and service reputation is something that will be associated with you from the moment you start working there. So it's important to know what the media, investors, bloggers, peers, and the general public are saying. Some places you should consider looking:

- News coverage.
- Bloggers on the industry as well as the specific organization.
- Customer feedback sites.
- Business, industry, and professional journals.
- The Better Business Bureau.
- Your Career Network.

Chapter 19

Be the Solution to Their Problem

When an organization decides to hire a new employee it's usually because of one of three reasons:

1) Someone recently left, was promoted, or was fired from the organization.

2) The workload is greater than the amount the current employees can reasonably manage. Because of this, the team is not working as successfully as it could be, and a new team member is needed to spread out the amount of work and help the company become more successful.

3) The company feels like it's missing a certain set of hard or soft skills that are needed to create efficiencies, have a more cohesive team, grow the business, or add a capability where none previously existed. In this case, the company needs to bring someone on board who can address this lack.

In any of these cases, the company has one singular goal—**to solve the pain of having an unfilled spot on the team.**

The day I showed up at Disney to interview for my first Hollywood job, I knew I was going to be meeting with the movie's director, Thom Eberhardt. I did my preparation, and arrived at my interview with printouts of some things I had done to help John Schlesinger during the *Madame Sousatska* shoot. One item in particular piqued Thom's interest.

During pre-production John would visit each location to pre-determine how he was going to shoot a particular scene. I'm a visual person, so instead of taking notes about camera placement on the script pages, I drew floor plans and marked camera positions at the appropriate spots. John loved these drawings because they jogged his memory of how he wanted to shoot the scene.

Thom loved these drawings too. He could envision how it would *make his life easier* as he planned and shot the movie *Gross Anatomy*. In "solving his pain," I landed the job.

How You Can Help Solve Their Pain

Hiring new people is a costly and time-consuming process. Hiring managers want to get the right person on the team as quickly and efficiently as possible.

You job is to demonstrate that you can put an end to their search, and allow them to get back to their own work. How? By devising ways that you can help solve their pain.

You might not have directly related experience like I did at Disney, but you can take what you know about the situation and create scenarios that will get your interviewer sighing with relief. For example:

- If you're applying for a job as a sales associate, you might tell a story about how you came to love cold calling.

- When interviewing for a job as a product manager, you could talk about a code check-in system that you found indispensable in your last job.

- An applicant for a job as an executive assistant might demonstrate a knack for juggling ten balls in the air at once.

Ligia's story provides a great example.

Ligia is a consultant who specializes in helping companies solve difficult sales and marketing challenges, particularly in the healthcare industry.

Several years ago, Ligia was introduced to a company that produced medical information booklets that provided illness-specific content for doctors and their patients. The company was having a problem covering the costs of getting the booklets distributed to the doctors' offices where they were needed most.

Ligia did her research. She understood the challenge the company was facing, explored options, and had a potential scenario planned.

When she sat down with the CEO, she presented her idea: What if they could get the booklet production and distribution costs covered by partnering with the pharmaceutical companies who produced the drugs used in treating each illness?

This solution presented a win-win for the pharmaceutical companies and the booklet producer. As for Ligia, she so adeptly showed how she could solve her client's pain, that she was immediately hired to devise a marketing plans and executive on the sales strategy that she had proposed.

You are no different from Ligia. You know how to do research and you know the specific job you are applying for. Now put the pieces together and figure out how make yourself an invaluable contributor who can *help solve their pain.*

This isn't magic.

And even if their specific "pain" isn't clear to you, know that there are many things you can do and say that will show your interviewer how you your smarts and work ethics can make their job easier. Every hiring manager likes to hear this, so if it's true, feel free to brag about it. A little gracious boasting can do a lot for your prospects.

Chapter 20

Be a Great Person

Let's face it. You might be the most skilled, most experienced and most qualified candidate, but that doesn't mean you're going to get the job. At the end of the day, the chosen candidate needs to possess both professional chops and personal qualities that match what the company is looking for.

This means that you need to become the kind of person that makes the hiring manager turn to your next interviewer and whisper, "You gotta meet this guy... he's a Great Person."

Think about it. How many times have you heard someone say, "We just hired this guy because he's a real jackass?" Probably not that many. And here's how this fits into Being Prepared When Luck Strikes.

People *Buy* People

They don't *buy* skills, or degrees, or accomplishments. They *buy* people. If you can develop your greatness as a person, more people will *buy* you.

So what is this mythic creature called the Great Person? Yes, it involves being decent, and honest and kind—all of the things you learned in kindergarten. But being a Great Person at work is so much more than that.

In fact greatness means different things in different industries. Being a Great Person at a law firm might be vastly different than being a Great Person at an advertising agency.

So why is this important? Because when given the choice between two candidates—one with perfectly matched skills but not so Great, and one with competent skills and quite Great—most hiring managers will choose the Great Person.

In *Good to Great* (which I mentioned earlier in reference to understanding you Contribution Style), Jim Collins addresses this Great Person concept in a chapter called, "First Who...Then What." Collins and his team of researchers learned that companies that were making the leap from goodness to greatness understood the importance of having the "right people on the bus".

These great companies "first got the right people on the bus (and the wrong people off the bus) and then figured out where to drive it." What Collins and his team learned was that the people on the bus made the company, not the other way around.

That's where you come in. **You want to be asked to board the bus.**

You want people to think that you'll be a valuable contributor to the team, no matter what role you're asked to play. And that's when being a Great Person counts the most.

Meet Diane. Diane is the consummate Great Person. And although she has been at her insurance job with Liberty Mutual for over twenty-five years, you'd think that she had worked at a series of start-ups.

Diane is smart, skilled, detail oriented, and steady. She works hard, is constantly pushing herself to learn new things (during her tenure, she enrolled in night school and earned her MBA), and her colleagues respect her.

Diane is constantly being offered new jobs, but not in the way you think. In an employment environment, where people change companies as a form of career advancement, Diane has never needed to. She keeps receiving new job offers *within* Liberty Mutual

People at Liberty believe that Diane is an invaluable contributor to any team she joins. From new initiatives to clean-up operations, she has been approached time and again by managers within the company about moving to a new division, tackling a difficult territory, or taking on new responsibilities.

Diane doesn't always possess a particular skill that makes her the ideal candidate for a role. What she possesses is a hunger for new learning, the desire to challenge herself, and the confidence that no matter how hard a job task or challenge appears to be, she can figure it out and make everything work.

Diane's skills are not what make her a Great Person. It is her ability as a valuable contributor that has managers at Liberty vying to *get her on their bus.*

So how do you make sure you get asked to board the bus? The best way is to make sure you know not only what Greatness means to you, but, more importantly, what Greatness means to the people who might want to hire you.

In the exercise that follows, you'll have a chance to find out what being a Great Person means in your field of interest. You'll have a chance to reach out to some of your industry contacts, get their advice and have a good excuse for reconnecting. It's also your chance to practice being a Great Person. So take this task seriously. It really can be a game-changer.

Chapter 20 Exercises

What does Greatness mean?

Greatness is different across industries. What the legal community thinks is Great is vastly different from what the advertising industry thinks is Great. It's essential that you get to know what people in your field consider to be the essential components of a Great Person.

As you go through this exercise, keep in mind that **success does not equal greatness**. A lawyer might never lose a case, but that alone doesn't mean he is a Great Person. A movie producer might make hit after box office hit, but that alone does not make her a Great Person. A guy you have drinks with on Friday nights might be the life of the party, but that alone does not make him a Great Person. Find out from your Career Network what qualities they think make a person Great in your field.

In parallel, it's important for you define what Greatness means to you personally. Let's get started.

- Take out a pen and some paper and make a list of all of the things that make you a Great Person. Below is a list of things that I consider Great in my work, and I look for these types of qualities when I hire someone to work with me. Notice that these are not skills, but personality characteristics.
    - Smart
    - Competent
    - Curious

- Enthusiastic
- Trustworthy
- Inventive
- Creative
- Resourceful
- Funny
- Doesn't take themselves too seriously.
- The ability to address a problem before I know it exists.
- Capable of anticipating my needs.
- Ability to define and execute on their work with minimal input from me.
- Up on current events and pop culture.
- I like them both personally and professionally.

Now it's your turn. Don't be shy. No one needs to ever, ever see this list.

- Next, make a list of three people from your Career Network who work in your field of interest.

- Compose an email, or prep yourself for a phone conversation, where you can request their advice on what it means to be a Great Person in their line of work.

- Make contact, listen carefully, ask questions, take notes and learn.

- Last, compare the lists and consider some qualities you might want to work on developing.

- Make sure that when you are preparing for an interview, you know your Great Person qualities, and are ready to put them on display.

Chapter 21

Interview Strategies That Get You Hired

Okay, you've done your preparation. You know your stories, you've researched the organization, you have ideas about how to help solve their pain and you've learned what types of people they consider Great.

These are all crucial steps in your path to getting hired. Next you need to take all of these winning strategies and turn them into a winning interview.

Though some of the sections in this chapter may seem obvious, nerves have a funny way of making us forget even the most basic things. So here are some things you can do to help you nail the interview.

Confirm Your Appointment the Day Before

By confirming your interview appointment by phone or email, you're demonstrating enthusiasm and professionalism.

- Twenty-four hours prior to your allotted time, make a call or send an email to your contact person and confirm the time, date, and location of the meeting.

- If you have questions about how to get there or where to park, this is the time to ask. Get your contact's direct dial information and the main number for the company, just so you have them handy.

- Close your conversation/email by stating that you're enthusiastic about the meeting (even if your nerves want to say you're not!) and are looking forward to learning more about the opportunity.

Know Where You're Going and How You're Getting There

I don't care if you're the most on-time person in the whole world. You can never be too early for a first interview. And "early" means that you've anticipated all of the things that could possibly go wrong in getting to your appointment at the agreed upon time.

- Whether you are driving, taking public transit or walking, make sure that you're aware of train schedules, driving times, traffic problems, road construction, and weather conditions that might prevent you from arriving *early* for your interview.

- Plan to arrive at your interview location *at least fifteen minutes early*.

- Several days before your interview make a practice run.

  - Check on Google Maps to see approximate driving, walking or public transit times.

  - Add thirty minutes to whatever Google says—if Google says it will take 25 minutes driving, leave yourself 55 minutes to get there.

  - Make your practice run at the same time of day as your scheduled interview.

  - If you're driving, make sure you know where to park.

- Remember to bring the address and contact info of the person who's interviewing you. If you run into some unforeseen delay, make sure you call your interviewer and explain why you are going to be late (and it better be a really legitimate reason).

- Bring your résumé, a pad of paper and a pen to take notes.

Being on time for your interview appointment is mandatory. If you can't be on time for the interview, how are you going to impress the interviewer that you'll be on time for work every day? The key is to make sure you are prepared and have a plan.

Find Out in Advance Who Will Interview You

One of the biggest mistakes that job seekers make in first interviews is not knowing in advance who they'll be meeting. It's essential that you to know if you're meeting with a recruiter, human resource (HR) manager, or the hiring manager (the person you would be working for).

Get this information before you arrive at the interview as this person(s) is your audience and you need to understand who they are, and from what perspective they're evaluating you. Know that different types of interviewers are looking for different things. For instance:

- A recruiter will view you from a skills and experience fit.
- An HR manager will view you from a skills, experience, and cultural fit perspective.
- A hiring manager will view you from all of the above, plus your ability to get along with and integrate into the team, your ability to be a positive, enthusiastic contributor, and your ability to solve the hiring manager's pain that comes from not having someone in that position.

Spend a portion of your prep time learning about this person. Use Google, LinkedIn and other resources to learn more about them. Ask the people in your Career Network. Find out as much as you can. You never know when you'll find something you both have in common that can serve as a great way of making a connection with them during the interview.

Anticipate Their Challenging Questions

There are certain traits that every good candidate has, and in the previous chapters, we've covered many of them. But perhaps the single trait that impresses interviewers the most is when candidates are able to "think on their feet."

Interviewers love to see that you can quickly understand a situation and be able to think and react directly to address the issue.

Thinking on your feet is something that can be learned and is worth investing some time in, particularly if you're uncomfortable when put on the spot. It's common during high pressure situations, like interviewing, for people to become so flushed and overwhelmed that they can't focus on listening to the question being asked, or come up with coherent answers.

The best way to anticipate their challenging questions is to *paint yourself in their shoes.*

If you're interviewing for a sales position, for instance, and you're interviewing with the sales manager, imagine what kinds of challenges and pressures he is under to bring in revenue, grow new territories, or train a sales staff.

If you're interviewing for a technical position and are interviewing with the VP of Engineering, imagine what kinds of issues she has to deal with to deliver high quality, robust products on time.

These specific job-oriented types of questions are essential for you to think about. By working through some potential scenarios and painting some viable solutions, you'll differentiate yourself from other candidates.

On top of job-specific questions, and the stories you prepared in Chapter 17, make sure you take the time to prepare answers to some typical interview questions like those on the following list:

- Why do you want to work here?
- Why should we hire you?
- How did you prepare for this interview?
- Where do you see yourself five years from now?
- Why did you leave your last job?

There are vast resources for interview questions on the Internet. The more of them you prepare answers for, and then practice, the more relaxed you'll be in the interview.

Prepare Questions for Your Interviewer

At some point during your meeting, your interviewer will ask if you have any questions. Consider this your make or break moment.

The biggest mistake you can make at this point is having no questions to ask.

Here's why:
- It tells the interviewer that you aren't an independent thinker.
- It shows that you haven't done enough preparation.
- They might end up thinking you aren't very bright.

Asking questions is a sign of intelligence and self-reflection. Not asking questions is a sure way to get your résumé put in the reject pile.

In my opinion, there are three types of questions: Question Mark Questions, Conversation Questions, and Questions To Avoid Like the Plague.

Question Mark Questions

Some questions end with a question mark and others don't. These are the ones that do. Great Question Mark questions help you get very specific answers to very specific questions. For example, you might ask, "Does the company encourage and support further education?" or "Can you tell me about some of people I'll be working with?"

You also might consider asking about:

- Specific job responsibilities.
- Top priorities.
- What it means to be a successful employee.
- Who you'll be working with, reporting to, have reporting to you.
- Long-term company plans.
- Training and advancement opportunities within the company encouraged.

There a plenty of places on the Internet to find lists of good questions to ask of your interviewer, so take some time and make sure you've got all of your bases covered.

Conversation Questions

I call questions that don't have a question mark on the end Conversation Questions. This indirect way of asking a question allows you to learn more about your interviewer, the job, or the company as a whole.

For these types of inquiries, pick a subject you are interested in learning more about. You can then say, "During my research on the company I…" Consider ending with, "I was wondering if you could tell me more about (the subject you're interested in).

Be prepared with a few pre-selected topics. And make sure you're actually interested in knowing the answer. Interviewers can "smell" insincerity.

With Conversation Questions, your interviewer get a chance to see your quick-thinking responses and you'll get an opportunity to see if there is good *chemistry* between the two of you, something that is essential in a good working relationship.

Questions To Avoid Like the Plague

Can you imagine starting a conversation on a first date by asking questions from a mental checklist that includes marriage, babies, religion and income? Most people would be completely turned off.

The following topics garner the same type of response in an interview setting:

- What are the hours?
- How much does the job pay?
- What are the benefits?
- How much vacation time do you offer?

- What happened to the last person who had this job?
- How long will it be before I get reviewed for a promotion?
- How did I do?

Here's why. These questions are taboo at this early stage in the process because they signal that you are more interested in the salary and benefits than you are in the job itself.

Greg made this mistake. His first question of his interviewer was about benefits. It didn't turn out well.

Greg wasn't an experienced interviewer, and he had his first baby on the way. Salary and benefits were top in his mind, and that's what popped out of his mouth when he was asked if he had any questions. Unfortunately, it was a fatal interviewing error, and Greg wasn't asked back for a second interview.

Instead of worrying about compensation, learn as much about the job and the company as you can. And know that there'll be *plenty of time for you to get all of your questions answered* if the process goes beyond this first interview.

Chapter 22

How to "Be" In the Room

If you haven't gotten it already from reading this book, let me say it one more time, in three different ways.

People *invest in* People. People *buy* People. People *hire* People.

From finding your "In" people, to growing your professional Network by 5s, to asking *favors* and getting people to help you, you have learned that personal connections are the surest way to advance your career.

There is no more important place to apply this thinking than in the interview room.

Despite your nerves, you are, if you've followed my advice, completely prepared for this. You know who you are and what you're looking to do. You're steeped in knowledge about the company and the people who work there, and you've developed into a Great Person. Now, it's time to bring it all together and have a great time.

Great time? Yes, you read that right. A great time. I mean it. If, for one moment, you can trick yourself into believing that this is just another conversation with another interesting person instead of as a job interview, you'll be in great shape.

The trick (and this is going to sound pretty new-agey and Buddhist) is to not be *attached* to an outcome, but just *be* in the conversation.

If, for one moment, you can turn off that over-active brain of yours and just be fully engaged, fully present in the conversation with your interviewer, you'll find that interviewing isn't as scary as your think it is.

Detachment is hard, especially for a smart, ambitious Career Artist like you. You've been working hard to figure out who and what you want to be in the world, and now you want to make it happen!

But you can't force these things. And the best way to get the results you want is to let things unfold naturally.

Interviewing is a Two-Way Street

Think of a job interview as you would a first date.

On "paper" the person you're about to meet for first time seems perfect. Good school, good job, loves their family. But just because they seem good on paper, doesn't mean they're a good fit for you romantically. There needs to be *more* for a relationship work. A first date is about finding out if there is potential for that connection.

The problem is that many first daters spend so much time scanning their "mental checklist" to see if this could be "the one", that they aren't really present during the date at all. This kind of first date rarely leads to a second date.

The same is true for interviewing.

Interviewing is a two-way street, where both parties are getting to know one another to see if there is a potential working relationship. Allowing yourself to be present and make a connection with your interviewer will give both of you the chance to have a genuine conversation. Hopefully, it will lead to a second interview and eventually a job offer.

So I want you to remember one very important thing: *you are not at the mercy of the hirer.*

You get to evaluate the opportunity for yourself and determine whether or not you think it's something you want to pursue. In other words, *interviewing is not a one-way street.*

Let's say this a different way, because it's really important for you to completely understand.

You get to evaluate the opportunity as well, and what you think of the company is just as important as what the company thinks of you.

The best thing you can do for yourself the moment before you walk into an interview is remember this simple fact. Because if it is true that People *invest in* People, then by the same token, you are investing in them as much as they are investing in you.

You want to choose a position because it's the *right* job with the *right* compensation, and the *right* opportunity to work with the *right* people—people who not only give you the kind of responsibilities and atmosphere you want, but also give you the kind of support and opportunities for growth that you need.

So do your best to think of your interview as a chance to meet a new person and talk about interesting things. This two-way approach will help you get to know the job and the opportunity in a much more relaxed way.

Kick off a Great Interview by Making a Connection

So now that I've convinced you that interviewing is a two-way street, it's time to get the interview started.

The best and most powerful way kick things off is to Make a Connection with your interviewer through a great opening, or Conversation Starter.

Choosing a Conversation Starter is more art than a science, so take a moment to read the body language of your interviewer before selecting a story to start with. I think you'll find that Conversation Starters are a great way of easing into a conversation, while simultaneously giving you and your interviewer a sense of each other's personality. It also allows you to see how serious, fun, casual or uptight they are.

You want your Conversation Starter to have nothing to do with the job opportunity at hand. Here are some you might consider:

- A topic from the news.
- A book you're reading.
- A memory associated with the building's location.
- The weather (as in, "I hope my daughter's ballgame this weekend doesn't get rained out").
- A photo, diploma, piece of art or books that you can comment on (asking about kids is always a good one if there a family pictures around).
- A shared club, alma mater or local sports team.
- A piece of jewelry or scarf that your interviewer is wearing (as long as it isn't coming off as flirtatious).

Don't be afraid to take the lead and kick off your meeting with a great Conversation Starter. It will grease the path into a more connected interview.

Sit, Listen, and Engage

The nature of an interview is incredibly dependent on the person who is conducting it. On one hand, your interviewer might be an interviewing expert who knows how to lead a fun, fruitful and informative conversation. On the other, your interviewer might be a novice who is as nervous as you are.

Because of the variable nature of your interviewers, it's essential that you help control the forward movement of the conversation. There are a variety of things you can do to accomplish this.

Sit Forward in Your Chair

Sit forward in your chair and lean into the conversation. This shows your interest, enthusiasm, and engagement with the person who's talking.

Listen and Look for Clues

Listen. And I don't mean only to the words that your interviewer is saying, but to the words "in between" the words that the interviewer is saying. Sometimes the most subtle clues are the most important ones, and can lead to good ideas for stories to tell, ways to connect and questions to ask.

Engage with Energetic Responses

Make comments. Ask questions. Show that you're engaged. Be energetic and interested. Nod your head to show that you're paying attention and use a strong voice when you speak. Let your interviewer know, from your words, actions, and enthusiasm, that you're fully absorbed in the conversation.

Create a Memorable Moment

At some point during your interview, you want to do something Memorable. Beyond your brilliant preparation, engaging, relevant storytelling and your skills and experience, a Memorable Moment can Paint you into your interviewer's mind, and you will stay there long past the end of the interview.

Doug Fleener, President and Managing Partner of the Dynamic Experiences Group, LLC, tells the story of a hotel guest who awakened one morning after a huge snowstorm to find that the hotel staff had cleared the snow off of every car in the parking lot. This simple act had such significant impact on the hotel guest that he told every client he saw that day.

Doug goes on to define a Memorable Moment in the retail business. "A Memorable Moment is created when a customer experiences something notable and impressive that makes a lasting positive impression. A Memorable Moment is something that a person will always associate with that business, organization, or person."

A Memorable Moment is crucial because once your interviewer has met with multiple candidates, the names, faces, résumés and experiences start to blur together. It becomes difficult to remember who is who.

By Painting a Memorable Moment, you create a *conscious lasting impression* that goes well beyond your interview. This is the feeling you want your interviewer to have as you walk out the door.

In the movie, *Legally Blonde*, Reese Witherspoon's character, Elle Woods, wows the admissions staff at Harvard Law School when she created a hilarious (and fairly inappropriate) video of herself to show why she would be a great law student. Elle went way too far, but the video certainly got her noticed (as did her perfume scented résumé), and in the end, they admitted her to Harvard.

I don't want you to go crazy like Elle did, but I do want you to think about how you can get your interviewer to say, "Wow!" when you walk out the door, and keep talking about you for the rest of the day.

So how can you create a Memorable Moment? Admittedly, this takes a bit of preparation, creative thinking, and panache.

- There are lots of things you can leave behind as a Memorial Moment.
  - An article you wrote.
  - A journal you thought might be of interest.
  - A marketing packet that includes printed materials from your past experience.
  - Printouts from your blog.
  - Anything you can think of that will remind them of who you are and why they liked you.

- A promise or "best wish" is another great way to have a Memorable Moment.
  - A promise to say "hi" to someone you discovered was a mutual friend.

- A promise to send some materials you discussed.
- A "best wish" on your interviewer's upcoming wedding, tournament, marathon or event that they mentioned during your discussion.

Even if you don't have a lot of experience, you can still create a Memorable Moment. Any effort on your part will show your interviewer how serious you are about this opportunity.

In the exercises that follow, you'll have a chance to take all that you've learned so far in this book and put it together in preparation for the best interview of your life. Know that you are ready, and that when the call comes, you will Be Prepared When Luck Strikes.

Chapter 22 Exercises

Getting Ready to "Be" in the Room

You've made it this far, so please don't run out of steam now. Before you head into that meeting, there are three important things you need to make sure you've got under control.

1. Interview Preparation Checklist

Okay, so the day of your interview is approaching, and you've got that horrible feeling in your stomach. You can either swallow an entire bottle of Tums, or you can use the following checklist to make sure you are so well-prepared that your nerves completely go away (well, almost completely).

- ☐ Paint Memorable Stories
  - ☐ The Story of You
  - ☐ The Story of Your Greatest Strength
  - ☐ The Story of Your Weakness
  - ☐ The Story of Your Last Job
  - ☐ Additional stories about your experiences, especially those that show critical thinking
- ☐ Do Your Research
  - ☐ Understand Their Objective
  - ☐ Memorize the Basics
  - ☐ Get Familiar with Who's Who
  - ☐ Define Their Customer
  - ☐ Investigate Their Competitors
  - ☐ Find Out Their Reputation
- ☐ Be the Solution to Their Problem

- ☐ Know How To Solve Their Pain
- ☐ Be a Great Person
- ☐ Know Your Strategy
  - ☐ Confirm Your Appointment
  - ☐ Know How You're Getting There
  - ☐ Find Out Who Will Interview You
  - ☐ Anticipate Their Questions
  - ☐ Prepare Questions For Your Interviewer
  - ☐ Know What Questions NOT to Ask
- ☐ Things To Bring With You
  - ☐ Your Confidence
  - ☐ Your Sense of Humor
  - ☐ The Address and Phone Number
  - ☐ Money For Transit Or Parking
  - ☐ Pad and Paper
  - ☐ Business Card
  - ☐ Résumé
  - ☐ Reference Sheet
  - ☐ Work Examples (if applicable)
  - ☐ A "Memorable Moment"

2. Your Conversation Starters

Before you head in for your interview, scan the newspaper, weather report and sports scores. Think of the book you last read, the movie you last saw, or your weekend plans. Come up with a few different Conversation Starters that will help "warm" the room.

3. Review Your Stories

Make sure you know your stories by heart. Practice them. Practice out loud. Practice with a friend, family, on the phone, or with someone you just met. Practicing in your head doesn't count. This is something you need to do with your outside voice. So find a guinea pig and start talking.

Chapter 23

Don't Just Sit There and Wait

Congratulations. You made it through your first interview as a fully formed, fully prepared person. I am thrilled for you!

You have learned who you are and who you want to be in your career. You've met lots of people and experienced how meeting people professionally can be fun and fruitful.

You've become skilled at researching companies and preparing for successful interviews. You've developed a series of dynamic stories that help alleviate your anxiety and draw people to you. You've been a Great Person and have done something to help them remember you. You nailed the interview. Now what?

There is NOTHING worse than waiting for that phone call or email telling you whether you're still in the running, or if you got the job. It's hell. But it doesn't have to be. And while you're in this stasis, there are plenty of things you should be doing.

Decide If You're Really Interested in the Job

Remembering that an interview is a two-way street, it's now time for you to *figure out if this is a job you really want.*

I know this seems odd to most people. As humans, we spend so much time wanting to be accepted by others (in a job search, a relationship, or in our families) that we forget that we have choices.

The question is: do you really want this job? What will you do if the company comes back to you with an offer and a great salary? Do you actually want it?

Think about the interview, what you learned about the company, the person or people you met, and about the specific role that you'll be filling.

Imagine yourself going to work there every day. The commute, what your workspace will be like, what you'll be doing, and who you'll be doing it with. Where you'll eat lunch, take a breather, make a phone call. Think about your expected responsibilities, and if you think you'll have boundless energy for them every day.

Go back to your Personal Career Brand to see if this job and this position truly fits with your Passions, Interests, and Skills. Do you see opportunities to grow there? Can you see yourself being there for at least two to four years?

These are really, really important things to consider. Try not to get so wrapped up in *getting the job* that you don't pay attention to *what the job actually is*. So please, re-read the previous paragraph and ask yourself if this is the job that you really want.

Depending upon your answer, the next thing you want to do is follow up with your interviewer.

Follow Up within 24 Hours

No matter how you feel about the opportunity, you ABSOLUTELY HAVE TO WRITE A FOLLOW-UP EMAIL WITHIN 24 HOURS. Did you notice that I wrote that in capital letters? That was to make sure you realized how important this is.

Why email? Although a written note is a nice touch, snail mail takes too long to reach your recipient, and in this electronic era paced world, that just won't cut it.

It is better to make sure your follow-up response is received in a timely fashion—especially in cases where the hiring decision is being made quickly.

What To Do If You Want the Job

If you answered "Yes" in the previous section, that you really do want this job, it's time for you to follow up with a *personal appeal.*

Use the 3-Act structure from Chapter 6, to write your Set-up, Purpose, and "Ask" email.

Consider mentioning something you discussed in the interview to help jog their memory of who you are. Give specific examples of why you are right for, and interested in the job, and make sure that you enthusiasm shines through. You should include:

Act 1—Thanks for making the time to meet.

Act 2—Your enthusiasm for the job and a personal appeal.

Act 3—Your eagerness to hear about next steps.

What To Do If You're Not Sure About the Job

If you aren't sure how you feel about the opportunity you should still write a follow-up email.

A second interview could help clarify any questions you might have, so showing your interested in *learning more* about the job is a great way to do this. Use the Set-Up, Purpose, and "Ask" format including:

Act 1—Thanks for making the time to meet.

Act 2—Your enthusiasm for the job.

Act 3—A request to talk again and learn more.

What To Do If You Don't Want The Job

If you know the *job isn't right* for you, you still should write a follow-up note. Why? Because you never, ever want to burn a bridge.

Even though you know the position isn't the right one, consider staying in the game so that you can practice your interviewing skills. To stay in the game, you need to *act* as if you actually want the job. Use the same Set-Up, Purpose, and "Ask" as above including:

Act 1—Thanks for making the time to meet.

Act 2—Your enthusiasm for the job.

Act 3—A request to talk again and learn more.

If you receive a request to come in for a second interview, go. It's good practice, and you can always turn down the job later if it's offered to you.

This advice might seem counter-intuitive, but you never know where that recruiter, hiring manager, or interviewer will be working next. By following through with the interview process and conducting yourself in a professional manner, you'll convey good business etiquette and make a good, lasting impression.

This could be useful down the road. By adding these people to your Career Network, you are creating potential long-lasting relationships for the future.

If you eventually find yourself in a position where it seems like you're going to be offered the job, you can tell them that *you're not sure if the job is the best fit for your career goals at the present time.*

Remember, you're the Career Artist here and it's perfectly okay to say "No."

"Follow on" Interviews

If all went well in your first interview, and you've been called back to meet other people in the company, you know your formula worked! Follow on interviews are meant to allow the company to build consensus around a candidate and get everyone on board with hiring the same person.

Follow on interviews are also meant to get to know you better and test out your skills at a deeper level. Employ the same techniques you did for the first interview. Have fun and don't be afraid to ask deeper and harder questions.

Swap you stories to keep it interesting, and if you need to repeat a story from your first interview, acknowledge that fact.

A variety of people might interview you. It's hard to know whether or not the person across from you has a lot or a little influence on the final hiring decision, so make sure you treat everyone with respect. You never know who might have the boss's ear, and you never know who might become your next "In" person.

Think of your follow on interviews as a chance to build your confidence as a candidate and an opportunity to hone your skills at telling your own stories. The more comfortable you get with yourself, the more desirable you become as a candidate, and the more jobs you'll be offered.

Accepting a Job and Negotiating Contracts

Congratulations. You've been offered the job! Your hard work and preparation have paid off, and hopefully you're thrilled with the opportunity in front of you.

Accepting a job is easy, right? You just say, "Yes!" If only it were that simple. There are a lot of details to work out as you enter into an employment agreement.

Depending on the size of the business and maturation of the company, your level of experience, and the seniority of the position you're being offered, there are different "negotiating points" that you can consider.

Because this book is about Creating the Career you have always wanted, and not the nitty-gritty of employment, I will not be going into a detailed explanation of contract negotiations.

However, here are some things that you'll want to at least be aware of before you sign on the bottom line:

- Responsibilities
  - Duties

- Required travel (if applicable)
- Reporting structure
- Performance review schedule
- Compensation
  - Base Salary
  - Commission structure (if applicable)
  - Bonus and profit sharing (if applicable)
  - Stock options (if applicable)
- Benefits
  - Health/dental insurance/family coverage
  - Personal and sick days
  - Maternity/family leave
  - Retirement benefits
  - Vacation and holiday time
  - Flexible working hours
  - Telecommuting
  - Severance package
- Other considerations
  - Signing bonus
  - Relocation expenses
  - Transportation allowance

There are plenty of websites that can help you through the negotiating process so don't fret. You'll be able to get through it. Visit my website www.carryapaintbrush.com to find some helpful links.

Responding to Rejection

Og Mandino, author of *The Greatest Salesman in the World* wrote, "Every defeat, every heartbreak, and every loss, contains its own seed, and its own lesson on how to improve your performance the next time."

Ah, rejection. Feels good, doesn't it? Sorry about that. People say that rejection is our finest teacher, but no one really wants to hear that.

What I say is this: Think of this experience not as a rejection, but as a *dress rehearsal* for getting the job you're truly meant to have.

If you have been employing the methods outlined in this book, it's just a matter of time before your networking, connecting, and preparing efforts pay off.

So here's the trick: Don't give up. "Sure, Susanne," you're thinking, "easy for you to say." But honestly, do you think that I, a former movie producer and screenwriter, and current software designer and new author haven't faced rejection before? I hope you're kidding.

At the moment when you decided to Claim Your Career as Your Own, you made a choice. You chose not to conduct your work life as business as usual, but as business as *you* want to do it.

In choosing this path, you're stretching yourself to try new things, have a different attitude, and make things happen in a completely different way.

And so, this one time, it didn't work out for you. I say, "Awesome!" Your next task is to figure out why it didn't go according to plan, and see what you can learn from the experience.

So here's what's next.

I want you to sit down with a pen and paper and think about what just happened. Take yourself through the following pages and see if any of these things resonate with you. Can you learn something from your instinctual responses that will help you understand why someone else was chosen, and not you?

I'm having you do this for two reasons. First, because we are ever-evolving human beings and the only species on the planet that has the ability to critically self-reflect and make adjustments to our behaviors when we want to.

Second, because once you have finished this short period of reflection, you're going to compose and send a note to your interviewers thanking them for their consideration and time.

Post-Rejection Reflection List
1) **Perhaps you weren't the right fit**
   Here's the truth. As hard as you may have prepared, as fantastic a job you did during the interview process, as much as they really, really loved you, sometimes there's someone who is just a better fit than you are.

   More often than not, your primary contact person will tell you exactly that. So I want you to remember that you were great. You did everything right, and you made a lasting impression. Sometimes it just doesn't work out.

Take yourself out to the movies, or dinner. Hang with friends and family. Feel confident in the fact that you've made some fantastic contacts who will hopefully become part of your Career Network for the rest of your life.

And don't give up. You were *this* close. And that means you're doing great. The perfect match *will* come. I promise.

2) **Ask yourself, "Did I really want this job?"**
   If you answered, "Yes," (and they did not give you a glowing indication that you were truly being considered), it's time for you to evaluate your interview experience.

   Was there anything you could have done to be a more appealing candidate? Think constructively about ways that you could have made your case more strongly. Think about places in the conversation where your answers didn't come out as clearly or convincingly as you would have liked. Think about skills you don't possess that they were looking for. Think about how you can improve yourself for next time.

   If your answer is "No, I didn't really want the job," then don't be disappointed with the rejection.

   Of course, I'd rather you be offered every job you apply for and *reject them* if indeed it's not the perfect job for you.

   Replay your interview in your head and see if you can indentify something that might have let your interviewers know that you weren't 100 hundred percent interested.

   Think about your body language, your level of enthusiasm, and the ways you answered questions. Did you come across as blasé instead of excited? Consider things you could have done to stay "in the game" longer.

3) **Ask yourself, "How could I have done better?"**
Was there something you heard from your interviewers that made you realize they were probing to see if you had experience doing a specific task? Were they looking for skills and experience beyond your current capabilities?

If so, and you want to stay in this field of work, it will be important for you to find out what you're lacking and consider taking a class or doing some volunteer activities that will allow you to strengthen these skills.

Did you come off as shy or stand-offish? Remember that People *buy* People, and interviews (though potentially one of the most nerve wracking things in the world) are your marketing opportunity.

If you think this was holding you back from getting the job, consider taking a public speaking class, or double-down on your preparation efforts next time, especially if you skipped the "practice out loud" homework in Chapter 17.

4) **Ask yourself, "What have I learned about myself from this experience?"**
Hopefully your answer is "A lot!" Each time you interview for a position, you have an opportunity to be your own observer and figure out what makes you happy, frustrated, nervous, or excited.

Review your feelings during the interview process. Did this job represent exactly what you wanted to be doing in the future? Or does it make you want to go back to the drawing board and re-evaluate your Passions, Interests, and Skills because it was so far from the mark.

Of course, these are the two extreme positions, and there are many in-between scenarios. Know that only you, as the experiencer, can explain what you learn each time you're tested during an interview process. And only you will know how to make adjustments moving forward.

Write a Thank You Email

To bring your interview process to an end you need to write a final email. It's just as essential for you to write a follow-up note to your interviewer when you're rejected from a job, as it is when you're offered a job.

Your professionalism will be noticed and there may be future opportunities to work with either the company or specific individuals in the future. Remember, these people are now part of your Career Network. Use your 3-Act structure to:

Act 1—Thanks for making the time to meet.

Act 2—Your disappointment that you didn't get the offer.

Act 3—Your hope that your paths cross again soon.

This last part is important because you want them to keep you in mind if they hear of any appropriate positions.

Put everyone you met in your Career Network database. Make contact with them on LinkedIn. Stay in touch. You never know where your next job is going to come from!

Lastly, please, don't bad mouth the company on Facebook. Don't write a nasty blog entry. Act with dignity and grace as you thank your interviewer(s) for their time and attention.

Thank Your Referrers and References

When you've landed the job (hopefully), or even if you didn't (better things are coming), send your referrers and references a note.

Nothing makes me more upset than finding out from a business colleague that one of the people for whom I had made an introduction had had a meeting without my knowledge. This is what I *call bad relationship management*, and it is something that could make your advocate decide to stop reaching out on your behalf.

Write to your referrer and express your gratitude for the introduction and tell them how things turned out—at every stage of the game, if possible. Thank them for their ongoing support and assistance.

Make sure you keep your references, even if they were never contacted, in the loop and express your appreciation for their willingness to speak on your behalf.

Part 5

Nurture Your Inner Career Artist: Let Yourself Evolve

The highest reward for a person's toil is not what they get for it, but what they become by it.

- John Ruskin

Chapter 24

Keep Your Paintbrush Fresh

This last section of the book is all about keeping your Paintbrush Fresh and will be especially important after you've been at your new (or current) job for at least six months. By this time, you'll have gotten your feet under you, learned the landscape of the company and have a good handle on your responsibilities and role in your team. So now what?

Career Artistry is about continually growing in your work life and adding new color to your palette. It is about bringing new and interesting thoughts and challenges into your daily world.

What does this mean? It means that landing that perfect job was only the first step in your life as a Career Artist! Now it's time to get some Fresh Paint and let yourself grow.

Take Initiative and Take On New Responsibilities

Career Artists make a commitment to themselves to have a career that is gratifying and fun. And I'm completely convinced that if you hadn't fully made this claim, you wouldn't have gotten to Chapter 24 of this book.

With that said, this is no time to rest on your laurels. Sure, I know that it took a Herculean effort to get to where you are. Meeting new people and growing your Career Network takes a lot of time and energy. The last thing you want to do now that you have a job is to think about improving the one you have.

But this is exactly the time to begin this process.

By constantly striving to grow at work, you'll keep the colors of your career fresh. By becoming complacent in knowing you're employed and simply performing the responsibilities assigned to you, you risk slipping back into the world of having a job, and not having a vibrant career.

A career is a moving, growing, evolving organism, and it takes plenty of care and feeding to keep it alive and thriving. So now that you're settled in at work, it's time to stir things up again.

Meet Ann. Ann was an executive assistant at a technology start-up located in Northern California. Her primary responsibility was to support and assist the company's CEO as he focused on building a brand new business.

During her first few months on the job, she learned everything she could about the company's business and came to believe that the company could be hugely successful. She decided that she wanted to not only stay at the company long-term, but wanted a position beyond her current scope. She wanted to participate in company decision-making, and she wanted to earn shares from the employee stock option pool.

With this vision in mind, she set out to make herself a great candidate for advancement within the company.

On her own time, Ann researched the company's industry and realized that she lacked the basic sales and marketing knowledge that would allow her to grow within the company. She requested to take a marketing course at a local university and her CEO agreed.

She also requested that she be able to attend important meetings as an observer as well as silently listening in on some of her boss's phone calls, all of which he supported.

Soon she was given a raise and asked to take on the added responsibilities of being the office manager. In this role she was tasked with finding new office space, so she set to work getting to know the vastly different needs of the engineering, sales, and product teams.

Over time, Ann became so enmeshed in details of the organization that she made herself indispensible. When Ann decided after six years with the company to move on, she left as the chief operating officer.

Ann's is a shining example of how to add *color to one's palette* and *grow one's career within an organization*. She came into the company as an assistant, and walked out as part of the senior management team. She achieved this by completely dedicating herself to her company as well as herself. She looked at each day as an opportunity to not only do her assigned work, but as a chance to look for new ways that she could grow her own skills and help the company at the same time. Hers is a great success story.

Unfortunately, not all situations will be as open for growth as Ann's was. In larger, more established companies, there is often a feeling that corporate hierarchy prevents workers from stretching beyond their bounds. These cases are truly unfortunate.

In general, the people who promote such bounded thinking are those who feel threatened in their own job security. Instead of providing opportunities for employees to grow, threatened managers try to keep workers down by limiting their exposure to upper levels of management and new, important initiatives.

If you find yourself in a situation such as this, I recommend that you skip directly to Chapter 25 and get out of that job as soon as possible, as it's most likely a dead end path for you.

"A Players" Hire "A Players"

Here's a harsh truth about the working world. "A Players" hire "A Players," and "B Players" hire "C Players."

What does this mean? It means that people who are talented Great People who are confident in their abilities ("A Players") want to hire and surround themselves with other people who are talented Great People (other "A Players"). This is because "A Players" delight in knowing that the people around them are ambitious and capable, will make their job easier, and will make them look good because the team as a whole will perform way above par.

"B Players," who don't feel as confident and talented as "A Players," tend to hire and surround themselves with people they feel are less talented and less competent than they are ("C Players"). They do this because sub-consciously it makes them feel superior, and they don't have to worry that their job is in jeopardy.

What does this mean? It means that sometimes there can be barriers when it comes to expanding your scope at work. If you have a boss or manager who sees you as a threat, then the chances for your long-term development are stifled, and it might be time for you to consider a Fresh Canvas.

Hopefully, though, you'll find yourself in an open situation as Ann did, where you're encouraged to take on more and grow.

Think about your current work situation and how you feel about it. Is the environment friendly and does it encourage colorful thinking and individual initiative?

If the answer is "Yes," then think about how you would like to grow within the organization. What can you do to add color to your job palette?

Consider the following as you make your assessment:

- Are there things about the business that you should challenge yourself to learn?
- Do you see any holes in company processes and procedures that you'd like to help fix?
- What courses might you take to fill in a gap in your skill set?
- Can you imagine any projects outside of your current responsibilities that you can do on your own time to demonstrate initiative?
- Is there a project that you can offer to lead so that you can practice and demonstrate your leadership abilities?
- Do you have any new ideas that you think will improve the company's products, services, sales, or marketing efforts?

Use your answers to the above questions as a framework for thinking about how you can *grow* in your job. Pick one or two of your findings and make a plan for how you can execute them. Talk to your boss to let him know that you're interested in taking on more, doing more, and learning more. In most cases, they'll appreciate it!

Find a Work Mentor

Author and professional speaker, Stephen M. Shapiro, can pinpoint the moment when he added fresh color to his work palette and changed his life forever.

Stephen was seven years out of college and working as a junior employee at Andersen Consulting (now Accenture) when he met his work mentor[3]. As one of 40,000 company consultants, Stephen felt like he blended into the woodwork and was indistinguishable from the other employees of the company. Then during one particular project he was re-introduced to something called "cultural transformation" work, and decided that Andersen's culture could use a little transforming.

Stephen was born carrying a Paintbrush and decided the best way to make this new idea happen was to place a call to Anderson's CEO. The CEO's secretary took Stephen's message, and word about the call got down to the partner leading Stephen's project about the call.

Instead of getting upset that Stephen had operated outside of the normal communication channels within their large hierarchical organization, the partner was impressed with his initiative and introduced him to Bill Stoddard who was looking into this kind of idea for the company as a whole.

Bill liked Stephen's pluck and invited him to come join his practice group. Together, they built a now well-known practice

---

[3] A work mentor is someone who encourages your growth within a particular company or organization. The mentor discussed in Chapter 5 is someone who can mentor you as you build your career as a whole.

called Value Driven Re-Engineering. Bill took Stephen under his wing and mentored him as the practice grew. Soon Stephen was traveling the world, not as a consultant for Andersen, but as an internal resource who trained Andersen employees on this new practice.

Training sessions and speeches led to his first book. From there, he stepped out on his own and is now a guru who speaks and writes about innovation and creativity.

Stephen found Bill on a fluke, but it was his boldness, smarts, and spirit that made Bill want to invest in Stephen's future.

In Chapter 5 we talked about getting a Mentor to help with your career development. A Work Mentor can do the same, and can give you assistance *inside* the company where your external Mentor might not be able to.

Finding a Work Mentor is one way that you can continue to add color to your work palette. It might be a boss, or someone you met on a specific project. It might be someone in human resources or the head of the company herself. Know that it may take time to find the right person, but once you do, you'll have valuable support in all that you're doing and looking to achieve.

Be Your Own Art Critic

As you move through your job, as well as your career as a whole, it's essential that you observe your own progress with a critical eye. Like an art critic observes, analyzes, interprets, and judges art, you can critically assess your progress in your career at any given time.

To do this you need to step back from the hold that day-to-day responsibilities have on you and give yourself the time needed to really think. Every few months or so, set aside a couple of hours for this process. Find a comfortable quiet place where you can reflect without distraction.

Take out your Personal Career Brand statement and re-read it. Remind yourself of what you wanted to be and do during this phase of your working life.

From a 25,000 foot level, evaluate whether or not your PCB still resonates with you. Are your Passions and Interests the same, or have they shifted or realigned themselves?

Over time, as we mature, I've noticed that our **Passions become more focused,** our **Interests expand** and our **Skills grow**. Take a moment to check in and make sure that your PCB still makes sense. If not, it's time to create a new one.

Reflect upon your job and ask yourself if it is growing *with* you. Has it expanded to include any new Interests, or has it endowed you with new Skills? Ask yourself if you feel fulfilled and enthusiastic about what you're doing.

If the answer is "Yes," then continue on your current path. You're making great progress, and you can skip to Chapter 25!

If the answer is "No," we've got a bit more work to do.

Consider what might be contributing to your lack of enthusiasm. Are you bored, stressed, or disinterested in your current work? These can all lead to reduced energy and job dissatisfaction.

Once you have critiqued your situation, you'll be able to better address some of the challenges you're facing. Here are some things to ask yourself:

- Are you feeling unsupported at your job?
- Has the job evolved into something you don't enjoy doing?
- Are you being forced to take on tasks that you don't want to be doing?
- Are your challenges something you have control over?
- Have you been delinquent in nurturing your career so that work has become repetitive and uninspiring?
- Have you stopped learning, yet didn't sign up for a class to take so that you can learn more?

I really want you to understand where your unhappiness is coming from, because some of these feelings might be caused by things that you can control and change.

Before you step away from any job, make sure that your dissatisfaction is not your own making. See if you can or should do things in your current situation to bring you back to "happy."

That said, you should never, ever be unhappy at work. Life is too short, and you have way too much to offer. Take steps to re-double your commitment to your current situation. Use the ideas from earlier in this chapter. Give yourself time to see if things improve for you.

If, however, you get to the point where you sincerely can't fathom working there any longer, it's time to move on.

Chapter 25

Sometimes a Fresh Canvas is What's Best

Despite our best efforts to keep a job alive and vibrant, colorful and inspiring, there does inevitably come a point where it's time to move on.

Someone once told me that you should "Stay at a job until it makes you physically ill. That's when you know it's time to move on."

I think waiting until you're "physically ill" is way too extreme. But there are other kinds of signs that you can look out for. I learned this for myself when I had my first "real" job, about thirteen years into my career.

I was living in San Francisco at the time and was hired by a direct marketing agency to help them understand how to build an interactive practice within their agency. The three-day assignment turned into a six-week assignment that ended up in an offer to come on board fulltime as a vice president.

Though I had been asked many times, I had never joined a company as an employee before. I loved building new things, and the life I had consulting to my diverse array of clients. And although I had played an interim executive role in companies many times, I had never taken the step to "go inside." Honestly, I was terrified.

But I really liked the people, and I really liked the work. I thought to myself, "It's an agency. There'll be plenty of interesting projects coming through to keep me engaged."

"Plus," I told myself, "It would be pretty cool to get VP stripes for my first "real" job."

The first nine months working at the agency were amazing. I had a great boss and my charge was to build an interactive practice. I spent time hiring new employees, building a great team, putting processes in place, training people how to build interactive products and coming up with great, creative designs. It was crazy and fast paced—just the way I like it.

One day I came into the office and everything felt different. My ten-person team was working like a well-oiled machine, all of the members doing their jobs beautifully and effectively. In fact, they were so good, they no longer needed me.

I started to feel like a fire hose—only needed when something went terribly wrong, and the team needed me to put out a fire. I became really unhappy and started dreading coming to work.

I went to my boss, the company president. He was a great guy and he ran the company like we were all family. He always said, "If you're ever unhappy here at work, come talk to me. If you want to get into something different, like race car driving, tell me, and I'll think about whether or not race car driving is something we as a company want to pursue. If it is, let's work together to make something happen. If not, we will part as friends."

So I went to talk to him. For a few months we tried a variety of different ideas to put new things on my plate. He worked with me closely, but in my heart, I knew it was time to go.

Leaving the agency was difficult, but I knew it was the right thing to do. It helped that I left on great terms after having made many lifelong collaborators and friends.

Sometimes a Fresh Canvas *is* what you need.

Committing to a life as a Career Artist means that you and your career life will be constantly evolving. You as a person are growing and changing. You are gaining new skills, new insights, and developing, modifying, growing, and transforming yourself. Which means the work you do needs to evolve as well. Your Fresh Canvas may take many shapes. It might be:

- A similar job at a new company in your same field.
- A higher ranking job at a new company in your same field.
- A completely different job in your same field.
- A similar job at a new company in a different field.
- A completely different job in a different field.
- Working for yourself.
- Going to school.

The possibilities for creating opportunities in your life are endless. As a concept, a Fresh Canvas provides you with the time you need to think about what you want to be doing next. These moments of change are exactly the thing you need to bring color, vibrancy, and excitement to your work life.

Leaving a job, or even getting let go from one, presents you with a huge, open world of possibilities if you choose to view it that way. Think of these moments as a gift—a time not of loss, but a time of infinite gain.

A workshop participant once expressed his concern to me about these moments of transition. He couldn't understand how a person (me) could move from one job to the next, or from one industry to the next without, in his words, "giving up all of the knowledge and advantage that you've gained."

I'm not sure why he thought you had to give things up in order to move forward in your life, but it got me thinking.

I've moved from professional theater, to the film industry, to the Dotcom world, to the field of social entrepreneurship, and into technology product development. Now I've written a career development book. Yet, I don't feel like I have ever given anything up. In fact, it feels like quite the opposite.

I feel like every place I've landed, everything project I've worked on, and every "dot" I've connected are the things that have enabled me to grow, learn, and take on new challenges.

Steve Jobs, founder of Apple, once said during his now famous 2005 Stanford University commencement speech, "You can't connect the dots looking forward. You can only connect them looking backwards, so you have to trust that the dots will somehow connect in your future. You've to trust in something—your gut, destiny, life, karma, whatever—because believing that the dots will connect down the road will give you the confidence to follow your heart, even when it leads you off the well-worn path, and that will make all the difference."

As a Career Artist, you have the opportunity to become an expert dot-connector. Bring with you everything you've learned, have done, failed at, and excelled at into the future with you.

Like a painter faced with a Fresh Canvas and a palette of paint, your possibilities are endless.

Chapter 26

Cultivate Your Career Network

The most successful Career Artists that I know have lots of people in their lives. Their Network by 5s contacts become friends, advisors, colleagues, collaborators, employers, and employees. With this kind of database, you never know who will introduce you to an opportunity that might change your life.

Stay Connected

Think of a Career Artist's Network as their circulatory system. It's essential that you keep this system healthy so that it can continually nourish you with fresh perspectives, new ideas, and fascinating possibilities.

For me, many of my co-workers and clients have become good friends, and although I have a professional website for my consulting work, it's not where I get my business. Almost all of my nearly 60 clients have come to me through contacts and referrals. Unttil I wrote this book, I didn't even have a website for my career coaching business.

The point is, even when you are a fully, happily and gainfully employed Career Artist, it's important that you stay connected.

Invite people from your network to drinks, lunch, a cocktail party, or even a charitable event you're attending. Send updates on how you're doing. Tell them when you've landed a job, changed jobs, or launched something cool. Email them articles that you think they might find interesting. Most importantly, stay in touch.

Meet Galina. Galina is a real estate broker and a master at staying connected with the people in her Career Network. Once a quarter, Galina sends a letter (the real kind) to everyone in her contact database.

In the letter, she describes current real estate trends and proffers advice to potential homebuyers and sellers. She includes a one-sheet Market Spotlight brochure that aggregates information and data about housing starts, job growth, and other economic indicators to help readers better understand the housing market.

Even during crazy real estate drops, Galina has been able to not only sustain, but to grow her real estate practice. And that's because she stays connected with everyone she knows.

Stay Organized

There are a million tools that you can use to keep track of all the contacts in your Career Network, but really all you need is a good contact database program and a good calendar program. Microsoft and Apple offer powerful desktop applications. Google, Plaxo, and others offer free online tools. Whatever tools you decide to use, it's incredibly important for you to keep your contacts up-to-date so that when you want to, or need to contact someone, their information is at your fingertips.

Use your calendar program to put reminders on your calendar to check in with people, and every time you meet someone new, add their information in your database, making sure to note down how you met them.

Lastly, please, please, please, DO NOT USE YOUR PHONE as your primary way of storing your contacts and calendar. If your phone is lost or stolen, your years of building your Career Network could be lost. If you use your phone this way, please ensure that it's backed up in a secure location. I would hate to see you lose all of your hard work because of a silly, preventable, mistake.

Stay Socially Networked

LinkedIn.com and the BranchOut app on Facebook have become the go-to tools for professionals to keep connected. When you meet someone new, remember to add them as an online contact. Both platforms provide lots of ways to connect to your Twitter account, professional events calendars, and much more.

A word of warning: If you are going to start using BranchOut on Facebook as a professional networking tool, I strongly recommend that you make sure your Facebook privacy settings are set to restrict who can see your wall posts, status updates, and photos.

Most hiring managers review your Facebook, MySpace, LinkedIn and other online profiles as part of their due diligence during the hiring process. Believe me, you do not want to have that picture of you dancing on a table to be the first thing the VP of Human Resources at Bank of America learns about you.

Some other ideas for staying socially networked:

- Set up a Twitter feed where you can post interesting and relevant updates about your work, your field, and your travels.

- Use online tools such as TripIt to let out-of-town contacts know when you're going to be in their city, and then try to meet up with them.
- Start a blog and become an expert and thought leader around a topic that interests you.

I suggest you take advantage of all that the Internet has to offer. But please remember to be smart about how you do it.

Setting Privacy on Facebook

To ensure that hiring managers do not see anything on your Facebook page that would make you look like a less favorable candidate, you need to adjust your privacy settings so that certain Lists and your public profile (which can be seen by non-friends on Facebook) have restricted access settings. Take the time to make sure that your personal information stays private.

Stay Smart

You've learned a lot in this book. About yourself, your vision of who and what you want to be in the world, and about your future. Don't make the mistake of getting complacent in a job, losing touch with your network, and then having no one to call upon when it's time to move on. Your Career Network is your lifeblood and it, like your career, requires care and feeding.

Remember these career-maintenance "Stay Smart" tips:

- Stay smart by staying in touch.
- Stay smart by meeting new people all of the time.
- Stay smart by introducing your contacts to people they might find interesting.
- Stay smart by posting things online in an appropriate way.

- Stay smart by learning how the Internet can help you stay connected, organized, and networked.

Perhaps the most important thing to remember is that *Career Artistry is not a solo sport.* It's more like football than snowboarding. Rally your team through great communication and ways to connect. Keep Your Paintbrush Fresh and your Career Network cultivated.

Chapter 27

Be the Artistic Director of You Own Career

In the theater, professional Artistic Directors tap into their creativity, people skills, management ability, and vision. They work hard, have enthusiasm, and inspire others to join them on a wonderful journey. In other words, they do many of things you have learned about in this book. Now it is your turn.

When you believe that the world is a blank canvas for you to Paint, amazing adventures can happen.

I was playing with my young nieces recently, when I found myself as a princess locked in the tower of a castle. While one niece tried to rescue me, the other, a fire-breathing dragon of course, blocked her way. Once I was rescued, I was shown the "local diner" where the former fire-breathing dragon was now a short-order cook. She made me a "grilled cheese sandwich."

Children are blessed with the gift of dreaming. They don't live in the world of constructs and of how things should be. To them, there is no "should." There is only what is and what they can imagine.

The intention of this book is to encourage you to find your own Bucket of Paint and Paintbrush and embrace your imagination.

Your career, and your entire life for that matter, is yours for the creating. Adulthood creativity doesn't have to be limited to piano lessons and weekend painting. Creativity is something that can be expressed everywhere in your life, and it's particularly valuable in helping you design and build exactly the kind of career you want.

Here are the 5 steps you need to follow to Be the Artistic Director of Your Own Career.

1. Claim Your Career as Your Own

Your career is rightfully yours and it's time that you assert your rights of ownership. Commit to this important first step, and change your working life forever. I invite you to visit my website www.carryapaintbrush.com and make the pledge for yourself!

2. Know Who and What You Want to Be

Discover the sweet spot where your Passions, Interests, and Skills overlap. Picture the kind of company you want to join, people you want to work with, and contributions you want to make. Find a Mentor. Communicate like a Pro. Know thyself and the rest will be easy.

3. Create Opportunities for Luck to Happen

Carry a Paintbrush wherever you go. You never know when you may need to Paint a Door. Meet great people, 5 at a time and get them to invest in you. Discover great opportunities by doing the reverse of what everyone else is doing. Work hard and luck will come your way.

4. Be Prepared When Luck Strikes

Over-prepare yourself and be a Great Person. Become a skillful teller of stories and understand what it takes to be present and make a genuine connection. Take a job because it feels 100 percent right and give yourself the gift of turning down a job because it's not the right one.

5. Let Yourself Evolve

Stay inspired. Stay connected. Grab your Paintbrush and a new Bucket of Paint when it's time to move. Enjoy the process. Let your inner Career Artist shine.

Rinse Your Paintbrush, Grab Some Paint and Keep On Going

You now have all the tools you need to create and re-create the career you've always wanted. Your Bucket of Paint and Paintbrush are always there for you—when you're in need of a change, when you're in need of inspiration, and when you want to get to know someone new. Just Paint a Door and change your life.

Remember that each time you reach for your Paintbrush, you're giving yourself the Opportunity to create your perfect next step, and it is all within your power to do.

So take a moment to grab your Paintbrush and thank yourself. The road you're about to embark upon isn't as well-travelled as many of the other paths out there, but I think you'll find it to be filled with amazing people, lots of color, and great adventures.

I want to thank you as well. I never imagined myself in the world of career and personal development, but this is exactly where I find myself. It's people like you, asking me to share my stories and techniques that have brought me to this point.

I guess I Painted a New Door!

I have no idea where it will take me next. But along the way, I look forward to hearing about your successes, your challenges, and your struggles. On my website, you'll find articles and tools to help you as you create your future. Come by and share your stories with other Career Artists just like you. You can find us at www.carryapaintbrush.com.

Works Cited

Chapter 1

Wiseman, Richard. *The Luck Factor*. Miramax, 2004.

Chapter 4

Collins, Jim. *Good to Great: Why Some Companies Make the Leap ... and Others Don't*. HarperBusiness, 2001.

Gibbons, John M. *I Can't Get No...Job Satisfaction, That Is.* January 2010. http://www.conference-board.org/publications/publicationdetail.cfm?publicationid=1727.

Kjerulf, Alex. "Yes, you can be happy at work." *www.csmonitor.com*. January 22, 2008. http://www.csmonitor.com/Commentary/Opinion/2008/0122/p09s01-coop.html.

Chapter 11

Wiseman, Richard. *The Luck Factor*. Miramax, 2004.

Chapter 10

Warden, R. *Reverse engineering*. Edited by Various. London: Chapman & Hall, 1992.

Chapter 11

Matthews, Christopher. *Hardball: How Politics Is Played Told By One Who Knows The Game*. Simon & Schuster, 1999.

Rosenthal, Lee. "Gofer It." *Details Magazine*, February 1994: 96-100, 134.

Chapter 14

M.D., M. Scott Peck. *The Road Less Traveled: A New Psychology of Love, Traditional Values and Spiritual Growth.* Touchstone, 1988.

Chapter 17

Obama, Barack. *2004 Democratic National Convention Keynote Address.* Performed by Barack Obama. Boston. July 27, 2004.

Chapter 19

Shapiro, Stephen M. *Goal-free Living: How to Have the Life You Want NOW!* Wiley, 2006.

Chapter 20

Collins, Jim. *Good to Great: Why Some Companies Make the the Leap... and Others Don't.* HarperBusiness, 2001.

Chapter 21

Shapiro, Stephen M. *One Simple Action Can Change Your Life and Your Business.* April 23, 2010. http://stephenshapiro.com/index.php?s=bill+stoddard&x=0&y=0 (accessed January 2011).

Chapter 22

Fleener, Doug. *Creating Memorable Moments.* http://www.dynamicexperiencesgroup.com/CreatingMemorableMoments.html. (Accessed January 2011).

Chapter 23

Mandino, Og. *The Greatest Salesman in the World.* Bantam, 1983.

Chapter 24

Shapiro, Stephen M. *One Simple Action Can Change Your Life and Your Business.* April 23, 2010. http://stephenshapiro.com/index.php?s=bill+stoddard&x=0&y =0 (accessed January 2011).

Chapter 25

http://www.freerepublic.com/focus/chat/1422863/posts. *2005 Commencement Speech.* Performed by Steve Jobs. Palo Alto. 2005.

About the Author

Susanne Goldstein is an engineer-filmmaker-consultant-web designer-business strategist-career coach who has spent the past twenty-five years helping organizations and people of every color and stripe be successful.

With deep expertise in storytelling, product development, user experience design and technology, Susanne has consulted to variety of clients including Walt Disney Studios, Microsoft, OpenTable, and Harvard University.

Her many happy career coaching clients inspired her to write this book.

Susanne holds a B.S. in Mechanical Engineering and an A.B. in Theatre and Film Studies, both from Cornell University, as well as a Masters in Public Administration from Harvard's Kennedy School.

She writes frequently about creativity and career development at www.carryapaintbrush.com.